Žižek and Theology

Žižek and Theology

Adam Kotsko

t&t clark

Published by T&T Clark
A Continuum imprint
The Tower Building, 11 York Road, London SE1 7NX
80 Maiden Lane, Suite 704, New York, NY 10038

www.continuumbooks.com

All rights reserved. No part of this publication may be reproduced or transmitted in any form or by any means, electronic or mechanical, including photocopying, recording or any information storage or retrieval system, without permission in writing from the publishers.

Copyright © Adam Kotsko, 2008

Adam Kotsko has asserted his right under the Copyright, Designs and Patents Act, 1988, to be identified as the Author of this work.

British Library Cataloguing-in-Publication Data
A catalogue record for this book is available from the British Library

ISBN-10: PB: 0-567-03245-0

ISBN-13: PB: 978-0-567-03245-4

Typeset by Kenneth Burnley, Irby, Wirral, Cheshire
Printed on acid-free paper in Great Britain by MPG Books Ltd, Bodmin, Cornwall

Contents

Acknowledgements	vii
Introduction: A materialist theology?	**1**
The approach of this book	3
Hegel	8
Lacan	13
Marx	16
1 Ideology critique	**19**
Ideology in practice	21
The challenge of cynicism	26
Ideology and the big Other	28
The stumbling block of the Real	31
Keeping enjoyment at bay	34
Liberal democracy and nationalism	38
2 Subjectivity and ethics	**43**
The Real as sexual difference	46
The 'vanishing mediator'	51
Fantasy and the big Other	55
Diagnosing ethics	60
The cure	65
3 The Christian experience	**71**
Prefiguring the theological turn	74
A politics of truth	77
The reign of perversion	83
Job and Judaism	88
Cross and collective	93
Love beyond the law	96

Contents

4 Dialectical materialism, or the philosophy of freedom — **101**

    What is dialectical materialism? — 103
    Self-consciousness as short circuit — 108
    The anti-adaptive animal — 113
    Theological materialism — 118
    The politics of refusal, or waiting on the Holy Spirit — 123

5 Theological responses — **129**

    An inventory of theological themes — 130
    Responses from Radical Orthodoxy — 133
    Other theological responses — 137
    Žižek's 'method of correlation' — 141
    Žižek and tradition — 145
    Religionless Christianity and the death of God — 149

Notes — 155
Index — 171

Acknowledgements

I would like to thank Ted Jennings, who first encouraged me to undertake this project and who read and commented on multiple drafts at all stages – a better doctoral adviser cannot be imagined. Brad Johnson also responded to all drafts and served as an invaluable, and long-suffering, sounding board on all aspects of this project. I would also like to thank the following people for their help at various points in this process: Michael Bérubé, Bill Brower, Young-Ho Chun, Joshua Davis, Jodi Dean, Scott McLemee, Tedra Osell, Eric Santner and Karl James Villarmea; my editor, Thomas Kraft; the staff of the Hammond Library at the Chicago Theological Seminary; and my family.

Introduction

A materialist theology?

In the early years of the twenty-first century, Slavoj Žižek became famous. He had been a widely discussed figure in certain English-speaking academic circles for over ten years at that point, ever since the publication of his break-out work, *The Sublime Object of Ideology* (1989).[1] As political events in the United States and around the world began once more to seem urgent after the relative calm of the 1990s, however, Žižek started to become famous in a different way. More than an academic celebrity, he became a public intellectual, following his popular response to the 9/11 attacks, *Welcome to the Desert of the Real*,[2] with a series of political essays on seemingly every pressing issue, in seemingly every possible forum: *The New York Times*, *The London Review of Books*, *In These Times*, even *Foreign Policy*. Beyond that, his many public lectures drew overflow crowds, and he was the subject of a documentary film, entitled simply *Žižek!* (2005), and of another film called *The Pervert's Guide to Cinema* (2006), in which he provides commentary on scenes from his favourite movies. All in all, he was attaining a level of notoriety, and even of celebrity, normally unimaginable for philosophers. Indeed, after the death of Jacques Derrida in 2004, he arguably became not only the most famous living philosopher, but perhaps the *only* properly famous living philosopher.

As a result of his increasingly high profile, recent years have seen a number of introductory volumes on Žižek's thought. Like those books, mine is motivated in part by the growing demand for help in getting up to speed on Žižek's complex and voluminous body of work. Its more immediate occasion, however, is one particular aspect of Žižek's output in those years: as his fame has grown, so has his interest in theology. His engagement with theology began in a serious way with *The Ticklish Subject* (1999), where he devoted a full chapter to a critical response to Alain

1

Badiou's book *Saint Paul: The Foundation of Universalism*.³ In the years that followed, he wrote no fewer than three books – *The Fragile Absolute* (2000), *On Belief* (2001) and *The Puppet and the Dwarf* (2003) – on Christianity, and his self-described 'magnum opus', *The Parallax View* (2006), contains an entire chapter and many other lengthy passages dealing with theology.⁴ Coming from an avowed atheist, materialist and Marxist, such a move is perhaps surprising. Lest anyone suspect him of a spiritual awakening, however, Žižek not only insists on his continued materialist orientation, but goes on the offensive:

> My claim here is not merely that I am a materialist through and through, and that the subversive kernel of Christianity is accessible also to a materialist approach; my thesis is much stronger: this kernel is available *only* to a materialist approach – and vice versa: to become a true dialectical materialist, one should go through the Christian experience.⁵

The goal of this book is ultimately to clarify the stakes of this thesis: what exactly Žižek's practice of a materialist theology entails, what brings him to theology, and what his work might mean for theologians.

A necessary first step is to clarify who Žižek is, beyond being a well-known philosopher who happens to have written a lot on theology. Born in 1949 in Ljubljana, Slovenia (at the time part of Yugoslavia), Žižek lived for most of his life under the Yugoslav variant of Communism known as 'self-management'. Already as a teenager, Žižek wanted to be a philosopher, and he seemed to be on track for a university position until his career was derailed by the university authorities, who deemed his Master's thesis on French structuralism potentially subversive. After several years, he was eventually offered a job as a researcher in the Institute for Sociology at the University of Ljubljana in 1979, a position he still holds. This post carried with it no teaching responsibilities – indeed, the regime wanted to keep him from having any influence on impressionable young minds – and so he was able to follow his research interests wherever they led, including into the film archives where he was able to view uncensored foreign

Introduction: A materialist theology?

films.[6] During this period, he was involved in a wide circle of Slovenian Lacanians, who were busy developing their own distinctively philosophical appropriation of Lacan.[7] In 1981, he made his way to Paris, where he studied under Jacques-Alain Miller, the leading disciple of the late French psychoanalyst Jacques Lacan, and earned a second doctorate in psychoanalysis. In 1985, he returned to Slovenia and became a leading voice in the growing democratic movement there and, in 1990, he ran for the country's four-person presidency on the Liberal Democratic ticket, coming in fifth place.[8]

Žižek's life since that time has been an uninterrupted flurry of academic activity – writing dozens of books in several languages, editing both individual essay collections and several book series, receiving a wide array of visiting professorships, and giving many successful lecture tours. More than anything else, this manic energy seems to me to account for much of his wide appeal, though other explanations have been proposed. For instance, unlike most academics, Žižek tells jokes, including vulgar ones, and he frequently uses examples from popular films. These traits doubtless do make his work more immediately inviting, but those seeking jokes or movies could more easily fulfil their desires by going to a comedy club or simply watching a movie. The true fascination with Žižek stems, in my view, from the sheer intensity that is most visible in his public lectures but comes out almost as clearly in his writing: one cannot help but see that this is a person for whom theoretical work is *the* most important thing. Commentators seem unable to resist talking about Žižek's own personal pathologies[9] – his tendency toward repetition, for instance, or his many 'nervous tics'. His greatest pathology, however, is his compulsion to do philosophy, a pathology he has apparently made no effort to cure or even mitigate.

The approach of this book

The bulk of this book is given over to a general overview of Žižek's thought from *The Sublime Object of Ideology* to *The Parallax View*, with a special focus on understanding and contextualizing his turn to theology within the trajectory of his work. In an ideal world, I would perhaps be able to skip straight to Žižek's books on Christianity, but as anyone who has attempted to read one of those books without much preexisting knowledge of Žižek knows, such a procedure is not realistic. Putting aside Žižek's idiosyncratic approach to organizing a text, the primary obstacle to understanding is the sense of having walked into the middle of a conversation – a very long and complicated one. Žižek does make some effort, particularly in *The Puppet and the Dwarf*, to help readers catch up with some of his central concepts, but the expository passages are summaries rather than true explanations, and the overall effect is to compound the confusion. Even if one is able to follow the basic outlines of Žižek's explanation of the concept of the Real, for example, the role of that explanation in his overall argument is necessarily unclear to the uninitiated.

The problem is deeper than simple unfamiliarity with the concepts Žižek is working with: the more fundamental issue is understanding how he is putting them together and to what end. Faced with this problem, some commentators have concluded that Žižek's approach is haphazard and even random. In this view, Žižek has a kind of 'grab bag' of concepts and examples that he applies to whatever problem he happens to be working on, resulting in some real insights that nevertheless fail to add up to anything like a system or a consistent outlook.[10] At its most extreme, such a view of Žižek's work can lead to the claim that, for example, *The Parallax View* is a 'record of what [Žižek] happens to think about whatever happens to have crossed his cerebral cortex at the time of writing'.[11] Against this position, others have insisted that below the surface-level confusion, Žižek has a definite philosophical system that, once discerned, renders his work consistent and comprehensible.[12] To my mind, although the 'systematic' approach is closer to the truth, neither position is fully convincing because neither can ultimately give an account of why Žižek addresses certain topics or elaborates certain concepts in a given text or at a given point in his career. For the purposes of this book, such an explanation is absolutely necessary. Throughout much of his work, Žižek uses examples from Christianity as precisely that: examples drawn from a shared cultural heritage. At a certain point, however, he not only decided to write three books on Christianity, but incorporated

Introduction: A materialist theology?

his distinctive approach to theology into his 'magnum opus' — and so the obvious question is: why?

I contend that the only way to answer that question satisfactorily is to reject both the image of Žižek as haphazard dabbler and the notion of Žižek's work as expressing a more or less static system. In its place, I propose to give an account of Žižek's philosophical development, mapping out the trajectory that leads him to his theological turn and, subsequently, to a definitive incorporation of the work on theology into his project. To this end, I have divided Žižek's English-language work into three periods, punctuated by two decisive shifts. In so doing, I am aware of Žižek's own warning against the dangers of periodization in *For They Know Not What They Do*: 'In such an arrangement [of a writer's works into periods] there is of course some pacifying effect, the thought is rendered transparent, properly classified . . . but we have nonetheless lost something with such a disposition into "phases": we have actually lost what is crucial, the encounter with the Real.'[13]

I will be explaining the concept of the Real at greater length, but for now it suffices to note that in this context it designates a fundamental deadlock that a thinker continually tries and fails to overcome, an elusive 'something' that a thinker can never quite capture. At the same time, in periodizing Žižek, I am merely following his own example, since few thinkers have ever been so fascinated by periodization. His work is full of attempted periodizations of Lacan, and in the same book in which he issues the warning quoted above, he proposes to divide the work of Ludwig Wittgenstein into three distinct phases, going against the broad consensus of scholars who are satisfied with only two.[14] I attempt to avoid pacifying Žižek through my emphasis on the internal instabilities and unresolved tensions in each phase that generate the shifts that inaugurate the next phase. If I do turn out to have fallen into the trap of overly tidying up Žižek's work, however, I still hold out the hope that my oversimplification will drive at least a few readers into a detailed study of Žižek in order to gain the satisfaction of proving me wrong.

My approach, then, requires a balance between comprehensiveness and focus. On the one hand, I must work my way through the whole sweep of Žižek's trajectory, tracing the steps that lead him to his engagement with theology. On the other hand, I must focus on the elements of his thought that are most necessary for understanding what he does with theology – the concepts and thought structures by means of which he attempts to discern the meaning of Christianity. As such, omissions are inevitable. For instance, the number of pop culture references per page is much lower in this book than in the average Žižek book, and I only examine one of Žižek's many references to film.[15] I have made some effort to supplement this lack by providing original examples, primarily, though not exclusively, from theology and from contemporary religious culture. There are also several aspects of Žižek's thought that I omit altogether, most having to do with cultural analysis or ideology critique, because I see his work on Christianity as having been occasioned by the tensions within his more strictly philosophical work on subjectivity, ethics and political theory. Accordingly, I have also focused the majority of my attention on Žižek's major theoretical works, as opposed to the books on film or other occasional pieces. Thus one potential test of the adequacy of my method will be the degree to which I have provided a framework that also helps readers to make sense of the texts I don't directly address.

This book is divided into two parts of unequal length. The main part is made up of four chapters in which I make my way through Žižek's works more or less chronologically, and that is followed by a concluding chapter in which I take stock of theological responses to Žižek and suggest potential areas for future research. Chapter 1 deals with Žižek's early period, during which he focused on the development of a new form of ideology critique based on the psychoanalytic theory of Jacques Lacan. The key tension in this stage is his support of liberal democracy, which I argue is incompatible with his approach to Lacan.[16] This tension reaches a breaking point in *Tarrying with the Negative* (1993),[17] where he elaborates a theory of nationalism that is simultaneously a devastating critique of liberalism. In Chapter 2, I continue my analysis of *Tarrying*, positioning it as a 'hinge' between the early and middle periods. Having rejected liberalism, but having yet to arrive at any positive political stance, Žižek spends his middle period in what I call a 'retreat into theory', developing in greater detail his theory of subjectivity and his often paradoxical ethical teachings. The decisive shift in the middle phase is seen in *The*

Introduction: A materialist theology?

Indivisible Remainder (1996),[18] where Žižek argues for a break with the fascination of 'subverting' an existing social or ideological order and a turn to the question of how a social order is founded in the first place. The tension, however, is that Žižek seems to envision all social orders as being structured in more or less the same way, opening up the question of why one would bother overthrowing a given order if the only possible outcome is a new order that can only possibly be different in degree, never in kind. In addition to providing an account of the path that leads Žižek to theology, both of the first two chapters introduce and explain the basic concepts without which Žižek's books on Christianity cannot be properly understood.

Chapter 3 begins by considering two passages from earlier works that seem to me to foreshadow the turn to theology, then turns to Žižek's encounter with Badiou in *The Ticklish Subject* (1999). Žižek's chief interest in Badiou is his theory of the truth-event, which offers the possibility of grounding a politics that would be something other than 'the same old thing'. He analyses this theory in light of Badiou's book *Saint Paul*, and the remainder of the chapter interprets Žižek's three books on Christianity as successive attempts to develop his own alternative theory of the truth-event by means of an alternative reading of the emergence of Christianity. His works on Christianity thus serve as a transition into his present period, as represented by *The Parallax View* (2006). Chapter 4 is devoted to *The Parallax View*, which is Žižek's most thoroughgoing attempt to date at developing a complete metaphysical system. Though Žižek's goal is to defend a version of materialism, theology nonetheless remains crucial to his project in *The Parallax View*, which is arguably even more consistently theological in orientation than his first two books on Christianity. I conclude my account of Žižek's philosophical development by giving some indication of the direction in which his project seems to be heading.

Chapter 5 attempts a partial assessment of Žižek's project from a theological perspective. After taking inventory of the primary theological themes Žižek treats, I summarize and briefly respond to the arguments of the theologians who have thus far written on Žižek. I then suggest two ways in which Žižek's non-theological work might be relevant to theology and conclude by drawing out the parallels between Žižek's theological writings and those of two of the most important theologians of the twentieth century: Dietrich Bonhoeffer and Thomas J. J. Altizer.

The main focus of this book, then, is the way that Žižek's thought has changed over time. In order to provide some basic orientation before diving directly into that development, however, I will devote the remainder of this introduction to the three figures who serve as constant points of reference for Žižek: Hegel, Lacan and Marx. My practice, here and throughout the book, is simply to take Žižek's word for it on his sources, rather than to attempt to provide my own supposedly 'objective' presentation of their thought against which Žižek's reading can then be measured.[19] Accordingly, my focus in these brief sections is on the main thing that, in my view, each thinker provides to Žižek: respectively, his style of thought, his major concepts, and his political commitments. Additionally, although this book does not presuppose a preexisting knowledge of these three thinkers, I provide some indications of good places to begin in their writings and in the secondary literature on each, as a service to my more ambitious readers.

Hegel

The German Idealist philosopher G. W. F. Hegel is the most important influence on Žižek's style of argument. Hegel is most famous for his use of the dialectic, an argumentative method that is normally broken down into three steps: thesis, antithesis and synthesis. In the traditional understanding, one first stakes out a position, the thesis, and then its opposite, the antithesis. The work of the dialectic is to bring the two together into a 'higher unity' – the synthesis – that incorporates the element of truth from each position while overcoming the contradictions internal to each. Hegel denotes this movement with the word *Aufhebung*, an untranslatable German term that carries connotations of both negation and elevation. For the traditional reading, the emphasis is very much on elevation. As a result, there is a widespread image of Hegel as advocating a continual process of collapsing all difference into sameness, culminating in a kind of 'happy ending' variously known as absolute knowledge or the end of history.

Introduction: A materialist theology?

Žižek takes the traditional reading and turns it on its head, placing an overwhelming emphasis on the negative as the true motor of dialectical thinking. In place of Hegel as a quasi-totalitarian figure bent on swallowing all difference up in sameness, Žižek argues that 'what we find in Hegel is the strongest affirmation yet of difference and contingency', and in place of a dialectical process that culminates in absolute knowledge conceived as full and transparent, he claims that '"absolute knowledge" itself is nothing but a name for the acknowledgement of a certain radical loss'.[20] Žižek's Hegel is a thinker of decisive breaks, of irreconcilable contradictions, of losses that are never recovered. This image of Hegel places the dialectical process in a new light. In place of the quest for a 'higher unity', Žižek views the dialectic as the process of a 'negation of negation'. A position or thesis is stated, and then another statement is made that, within the frame of the first position, appears as a negation or antithesis. The synthesis does not overcome the negativity of the antithesis, but radicalizes it to such a degree that it no longer appears as a negation. Put differently: instead of healing the break introduced by the antithesis, it completes the break by removing the frame within which it appears as 'merely' a break. Thus Žižek can say, '"Negation of negation" is . . . nothing but repetition at its purest: in the first move, a certain gesture is accomplished and fails; then, in the second move, this same gesture is simply *repeated*.'[21]

This basic three-part structure of the 'negation of negation' is pervasive in Žižek's writings. To illustrate it, I have chosen two specific examples from Žižek's writings, one religious, the other political. The first is found in *The Puppet and the Dwarf*, in a passage where Žižek is attempting to explain the meaning of Christ's death. He lays out two widely held positions:

> The first approach is legalistic: there is guilt to be paid for, and, by paying our debt for us, Christ redeemed us (and, of course, thereby forever indebted us); from the participationist perspective, on the contrary, people are freed from sin not by Christ's death as such, but by sharing in Christ's death, by dying to sin, to the way of the flesh.[22]

These two perspectives are familiar as, broadly speaking, the traditional or 'conservative' view and the 'liberal' view of the meaning of the incarnation. As Žižek points out, the 'liberal' view 'tends to deny the direct divine nature of Christ', presenting him as more of a model to follow.[23] Attempting to decide between the two, Žižek says:

> In the abstract, of course, the participationist reading is the correct one, while the sacrificial reading 'misses the point' of Christ's gesture; the only way to the participationist reading, however, is through the sacrificial one, through its inherent overcoming. The sacrificial reading is the way Christ's gesture appears within the very horizon that Christ wanted to leave behind, within the horizon for which we die in identifying with Christ . . .[24]

Here Žižek is making one of his most characteristic dialectical moves, pointing out a mistake that is nonetheless a necessary step in arriving at the correct position. In this specific case, the legalistic approach is clearly incorrect, and in fact Žižek argues that if we stay within its frame, 'Christ's death cannot but appear as the ultimate assertion of the law . . . which burdens us, its subjects, with guilt, and with a debt we will never be able to repay.'[25] However, if we attempt to skip *directly* to the 'correct' position, that position loses its punch. The true meaning of Christ's death is not immediately the call for participation, but rather the break with the legalistic view, a break which opens up the space for participation in a new kind of social collective outside the logic of debt and repayment. In fact, the participation perspective, properly conceived, is a kind of embodiment of the break with the legalistic perspective – without that persistent element of negativity, the cross loses its power.

The second example comes from *For They Know Not*, which is also the best single book to read for those who are interested specifically in Žižek's position on Hegel. Citing G. K. Chesterton's defence of the detective story, Žižek claims that law itself is actually the greatest possible crime and argues that Chesterton's insight exactly captures the logic of the Hegelian 'negation of negation':

Introduction: A materialist theology?

First, we have the simple opposition between the position and its negation – in our case, between the positive, appeasing law, and the multitude of its particular transgressions, crimes; the 'negation of negation' occurs when one notices that the only true transgression, the only true negativity, is that of the law itself which changes all the ordinary criminal transgressions into an indolent positivity.[26]

Later, he takes this logic a step further, again citing a famous Christian author, Blaise Pascal:

'At the beginning' of the law, there is a certain 'outlaw,' a certain Real of violence which coincides with the act itself of the establishment of the reign of law: the ultimate truth about the reign of law is that of a usurpation, and all classical politico-philosophical thought rests on the disavowal of this violent act of foundation.[27]

Responding to this passage, Jodi Dean supplies a concrete example: the origin of the United States Constitution.[28] The original intent of the convention that provided the impetus behind the new constitution was simply to revise the Articles of Confederation, the legal order that prevailed in the wake of the American Revolution. Instead, they thoroughly rewrote the document and, even more problematically, they developed a new mode of ratification – instead of requiring all thirteen states to agree to any changes, the new constitution would go forward with the approval of only nine. Overall, the entire process was illegal in terms of the existing law. As Dean says, the authority to found the law is only ever 'constituted retroactively'.[29] This logic is not limited to the United States Constitution: by definition, the imposition of a new legal order is always illegal. That is, it violates the previous order, but is not yet 'covered' by the order it founds. Following the logic of the 'negation of negation', the attempt to found a new legal order isn't a crime that manages to reach some kind of compromise or 'higher unity' with the existing law – it is a crime so radical that it undermines the standard that made it a crime.

Even more than his tendency toward digression, this dialectical style is arguably the single biggest reason that readers accustomed to the more straightforward prose style prized by the Anglo-American tradition have difficulty following his arguments. Learning to identify his dialectical arguments is thus one of the most important ways of getting a handle on what Žižek is saying. To assist in this process, I have tried to lay out relatively schematized examples of dialectical arguments at opportune moments throughout the text, but there are also some general cues to watch for when reading Žižek. For one, he will often introduce an 'antithesis' with a rhetorical question of the form: 'Is not the exact opposite the case?' His heavy reliance on rhetorical questions is often confusing, particularly when he later seems to presuppose an answer of 'yes' without clearly establishing it, but this habit becomes less distracting when the questions are seen as steps along the way toward the position Žižek will ultimately embrace. Additionally, Žižek often interrupts a position with ellipses (. . .), as if he is simply trailing off or getting bored with a given line of thought. Normally the ellipses will serve to introduce some kind of negation, making them another kind of signpost in Žižek's dialectical arguments.

Most of Žižek's extended discussions of Hegel are taken up with clarifying the true structure of the dialectic, often without reference to any specific text. The bulk of Žižek's favourite examples are taken from the *Phenomenology of Spirit*, and Hegel's own most detailed exposition of the dialectic is found in the *Science of Logic* – both of which are notoriously difficult texts. For first-time readers of Hegel, a good thing to keep in mind is that texts with titles including *Philosophy of . . .* are generally much easier to read, because they are made up of lecture courses. Among those texts, his *Lectures on the Philosophy of Religion* provides important background to Žižek's understanding of the incarnation. A somewhat more readable account of the dialectic can be found in the *Encyclopedia Logic*. To understand the reception of Hegel among the twentieth-century French thinkers to whom Žižek is responding, the most important text to read is Alexander Kojève's *Introduction to the Reading of Hegel*, an influential series of lectures on the *Phenomenology of Spirit*. The general introduction that I have found most helpful is Stephen Houlgate's *Introduction to Hegel: Freedom, Truth and History*, and a more advanced study that is basically in line with Žižek's reading of Hegel is Catherine Malabou's *The Future of Hegel: Plasticity, Temporality, and Dialectic*.[30]

Introduction: A materialist theology?

Lacan

The most visible authority for Žižek's work is the twentieth-century French psychoanalyst Jacques Lacan. Believing that the dominant trends in psychoanalysis had suppressed Freud's most important insights, Lacan undertook a 'return to Freud'. Though this necessarily involved detailed attention to Freud's texts, his goal was not to advance a kind of 'Freud fundamentalism', but rather to uncover and reformulate the core concepts implied by Freud's discoveries. In a series of dense writings – or *écrits*, a French term for 'writings' that is often left untranslated when referring to Lacan – and, perhaps more importantly, in his famous seminars, Lacan brought Freud into contact with the dominant philosophical schools of his time, including structuralism, existentialism and phenomenology. The result is a formalization of the fundamental insights of psychoanalysis into a series of bizarre and paradoxical concepts, which are represented by symbols that, punning on the linguistic term 'phoneme', Lacan called 'mathemes' and then put together into various 'equations' or diagrams. A major goal of Žižek's early works is to render these concepts and diagrams comprehensible,[31] most famously through his use of examples from film.

It is difficult, if not impossible, to determine where Lacan's influence ends and Hegel's begins for Žižek. His explicit statements emphatically put Lacan in the driver's seat and define his approach to Hegel as a 'Lacanian reading'. Žižek's reading of Hegel, with its overwhelming emphasis on negativity and loss, is certainly 'Lacanian' in the sense of fitting with the general ethos of Lacan's writings, which present a world structured around lacks, gaps and voids. 'Lacanian' though it may be, however, Žižek's reading of Hegel is not *Lacan's* reading, as Lacan came to embrace the traditional understanding of Hegel and, accordingly, to share the profound suspicion of the Hegelian project that has marked much of twentieth-century French thought. In order to show that his 'Lacanian reading' of Hegel is credible, therefore, he must demonstrate the compatibility between Lacan's concepts and the basic structure of Hegel's thought. In the early works, therefore, Žižek will often provide an explanation of a concept from Lacan, then draw a parallel from Hegel's writings, a strategy that is particularly evident in *For They Know Not*. This basic procedure tends toward an attempt to understand the internal contradictions of Lacan's concepts in a dialectical way – based, of course, on his 'Lacanian' reading of the dialectic – and, more generally, to show that Lacan had a 'Hegelian' style of thought even when he believed himself to be totally in opposition to Hegel.[32]

Thus a Lacanian reading of Hegel paradoxically requires a Hegelian reading of Lacan, giving rise to a potential 'chicken or egg' problem. In practice, over the course of his trajectory, Žižek's use of Hegel becomes limited more and more to the dialectical approach rather than to any particular example or passage, and his use of Lacan shifts from a general exposition to a focus on a handful of concepts that he develops in ways that ultimately move beyond Lacan's own usage. For this reason, my approach ends up to a large extent pushing Hegel into the background, dispensing with Žižek's Hegelian parallels and concentrating on an explication of the central Lacanian concepts and the ways in which Žižek brings them into relationship with one another. The major exception to this rule is the crucial parallel, which I explain at some length in Chapter 1, that Žižek draws between the structure of the dialectic and the underlying logic of the concept of 'the Real', which for Žižek is by far Lacan's most important philosophical contribution. My hope is that my relative lack of explicit attention to Hegel on the level of 'content' is balanced by the pervasiveness of the dialectical 'form' in the exposition of Lacan's concepts.

The first two chapters in particular are given over to an exposition of the most important Lacanian concepts. Since, in my view, those concepts can only be understood in their interrelations, I believe that any attempt to give brief 'definitions' here would only lead to unnecessary confusion. For those who are already familiar with the basic vocabulary, however, or need help with some particular concept, I will note the chapters in which the key Lacanian terms are explained:

- Chapter 1: the big Other, the master signifier, the Real, fantasy, *jouissance*, *objet petit a*.
- Chapter 2: sexual difference (the masculine 'constitutive exception' and feminine 'non-all'), the subject, the big Other

Introduction: A materialist theology?

(again), the psychoanalytic diagnoses (hysteria, obsession, perversion, psychosis), the psychoanalytic cure.
- Chapter 3: the discourse of the analyst.

With the one exception noted above, then, Chapters 3 and 4 do not introduce new terminology so much as show how Žižek continues to put the established concepts to work in new ways. Thus, though I understand that some readers may wish to skip directly to the chapter on theology, I strongly encourage them to be patient and to work through the first two chapters. Readers who have some familiarity with Lacan may also notice that there are certain famous concepts – such as the distinction between 'empty' and 'full' speech, the triad of the Imaginary, Symbolic and Real, and the 'four discourses' – that I do not address, even though Žižek does sometimes make use of them. The choice of concepts has been made partly out of economy and partly out of the necessity of focusing less on Žižek's expository work on Lacan and more on the ways he uses Lacan's concepts in his own project, most importantly in his approach to Christianity.[33]

The bulk of Žižek's references to Lacan are drawn from his seminars. The most broadly important seminar for understanding Žižek's work is arguably *Seminar XX*, on feminine sexuality, but *Seminar VII*, on ethics, is a very close second and is particularly notable for the purposes of this book as it includes Lacan's reading of Romans 7. *Seminar XI*, simply entitled *The Four Fundamental Concepts of Psychoanalysis* in some editions, is a good place to start for readers new to Lacan, as it was the first of his seminars that was open to the general public instead of being limited to analysts in training. His seminars are widely acknowledged to be easier to understand, though they are necessarily uneven and full of digressions, since the published texts consist of transcriptions of Lacan's largely improvisational presentations. His *Écrits* are extremely dense, but also much more focused. Since Žižek's reading of Lacan is focused more on his late work, many of the available secondary sources, which focus on the earlier 'structuralist' Lacan who was most important for his initial American reception, are likely to be confusing to those who wish to learn about Lacan for the sake of Žižek. For a clear introduction to Lacan's work that is broadly in line with Žižek's understanding, Bruce Fink's work is a great place to begin. His book *The Lacanian Subject* has a more 'philosophical' approach, for which his *Clinical Introduction to Lacanian Psychoanalysis* provides a very valuable supplement that is especially helpful in understanding the diagnostic categories.[34]

Marx

Of his three main sources, Marx is the one with whom Žižek has perhaps the most complicated relationship. On the one hand, it is clear that Marx is a decisive influence on Žižek's politics, which can be described as a set of resolutely leftist commitments grounded in anti-capitalism. Beyond that, Marx's importance to Žižek's theoretical work is readily visible in the first essay of *The Sublime Object of Ideology*, which analyses Marx's concept of commodity fetishism. One the other hand, Marx is arguably the least 'authoritative' of Žižek's authorities. One often gets the sense that for Žižek, Lacan and Hegel are always right, at least when properly understood, but he is sharply critical of Marx on a crucial point: the possibility of Communism arising out of capitalism. Although Marx is famous as a harsh critic of Hegel, Žižek argues that Marx's notion that the internal contradictions of capitalism will give rise to a higher social order called Communism is actually profoundly 'Hegelian' according to the traditional understanding – here Marx is presenting a narrative of progress where the destruction caused by capitalism will turn out to be 'worth it' in the end. Hence Žižek claims that in his critiques of Hegel, Marx is actually boxing against his own shadow. If Marx had been more *truly* Hegelian (in Žižek's sense), he would have recognized that what was necessary was actually a complete break with capitalism, rather than an attempt to keep the good parts while getting rid of the bad.[35]

In addition to Marx himself, Žižek also works with two important prongs of the broader Marxist tradition: the theoretical tradition of Western Marxism and the revolutionary tradition founded by Lenin. In his earlier works, his engagement with the revolutionary tradition is largely limited to an analysis of the ideology of Stalinism, which is a constant preoccupation across his entire trajectory. This analysis is grounded in his own personal

Introduction: A materialist theology?

experience as one who lived under a Communist regime whose founder, Josip Tito, took a Stalinist approach despite maintaining some distance from the Soviet Union. In more recent years, Žižek has also devoted considerable attention to Lenin, a development that I discuss at greater length in Chapter 5. On a theoretical level, Žižek's most important Marxist influence aside from Marx himself is Louis Althusser, whose theory of ideology is explained in Chapter 1. The French Marxists who followed after Althusser – a group that includes Alain Badiou – remain some of his most important dialogue partners on questions of political theory. Of the other Western Marxists Žižek draws upon, the most important for understanding his approach to theology is Walter Benjamin. I address Žižek's use of Benjamin's work in Chapter 3.

The majority of Žižek's references to Marx come from the first volume of *Capital*, though the *Communist Manifesto* has played an important role in more recent works. Essentially all of the texts Žižek uses can be found in Robert D. Tucker's standard anthology, *The Marx-Engels Reader*, which is also the best place to start in getting a basic understanding of Marx's thought. Additionally, David Harvey's *The Limits to Capital*, recently reissued in a new edition, provides an exceptionally clear exposition of Marx's critique of political economy, with a special emphasis on the dialectical character of Marx's argument. The key text from the French Marxist tradition for Žižek is Althusser's 'Ideology and Ideological State Apparatuses', which is included in the collection *Lenin and Philosophy*. The texts of Lenin most important to Žižek can be found in his own anthology, *Revolution at the Gates*, and those seeking a broader picture of Lenin's thought can begin with *The Essential Works of Lenin*.[36]

It should already be clear that Žižek does not treat his sources as 'hermetically sealed' entities – rather, what is distinctive about his work is the creative ways that he brings them together. For this reason, one could read his intellectual trajectory as a series of attempts to bring them together in a coherent and compelling way, and thereby to make their thought his own. Chapter 1 will deal with the first such attempt, centred on the question of ideology.

Chapter 1
Ideology critique

This chapter will discuss what I am calling Žižek's 'early' period, focusing on *The Sublime Object of Ideology* (1989), *For They Know Not What They Do* (1991) and *Tarrying with the Negative* (1993). Both in terms of the periodization I am using in this book and in terms of Žižek's engagement with theology, these early English works constitute a kind of 'pre-history'. This is not to discount their importance. They brought Žižek (and the work of the Slovenian Lacanian school in general) to the attention of an international readership. They also helped to rejuvenate the practice of ideology critique, the area of Marxist theory involving the analysis of the (false) ideas that help to support the dominant system. And in certain respects, these early books compare favourably to many of his later works. Perhaps most importantly for first-time readers of Žižek, they contain many expository passages, whereas later works tend to presuppose knowledge of Žižek's primary concepts and themes. *Sublime Object* is very often cited as his most 'accessible' book, and *For They Know Not* is a sustained effort of clear, patient exposition that has no real parallel among his other works. *Tarrying With the Negative* – in my view Žižek's most consistently satisfying work – weaves together popular culture and politics with a reading of German Idealism in a way that makes the precise relationship between Kant and Hegel seem like a pressing, immediately contemporary concern. Overall, these early works are simply enjoyable to read in a way that few books of philosophy or theory are (including many of Žižek's own later writings).

Žižek's stated project, beginning with *Sublime Object*, is threefold. First, he wants to elaborate Lacan's psychoanalytic theory as 'perhaps the most radical contemporary version of the Enlightenment'. For Žižek, this means that one must not conceive of Lacan as a 'postmodernist' or 'poststructuralist', but rather as a true philosopher in the lineage of Descartes and Kant. Much of his effort on this front consists in translating Lacan's often opaque writing into more straightforward terms. Second, he wants to reclaim Hegel by offering a Lacanian reading of him. Third, he wishes to introduce Lacanian concepts into the Marxist theory of ideology.[1] (In *For They Know Not*, he lays out this same basic triad, adding that there is a fourth element around which these three elements circulate: his love for popular culture.[2])

Already, then, we have Žižek's primary points of reference: Lacan, Hegel and Marxism. This trio will be a constant in his later work. The problem is that he has not yet managed to put them together in a stable and coherent way. On the one hand – speaking from the perspective of his later work – he does not yet seem to have fully 'digested' Lacan and Hegel, in the sense of being clear on what exactly he *wants* from them. On the other hand, his primary insights into ideology often seem to be more or less detachable from the Lacanian–Hegelian edifice. The phenomena he analyses can easily be put into normal, commonsense language: for instance, 'cynicism doesn't undermine the system – the system *needs* people to maintain a cynical distance toward the official ideology' or 'after Communism fell, people turned to nationalism to give them some sense of stability and identity in the face of global capitalism'. Many would agree that his insights into ideology are valuable in their own right, but we are still left with the question: why did we need Lacan and Hegel to get us here?

To justify translating these ideas into his Lacanian–Hegelian terms, Žižek must, in my view, demonstrate two things. First, he must show that such a translation provides clarity of analysis and that new situations are analysable in basically the same terms as they come up. Žižek's success on this front has been considerable. In this early period and beyond, he has shown that his approach is flexible enough to account for a wide range of cultural and political phenomena: the culture of cynicism, the resurgence of nationalism and fundamentalism, cyberspace and genetic engineering, and many others.[3]

Second, Žižek must show that his theory provides resources to tell us how we can intervene and change the situation. On this count, Žižek's early work fails – not merely in my personal assessment, but on his own terms. It is not that he fails to provide us with an answer: his initial proposed solution at this stage is liberal democracy.⁴ For Žižek at this stage, liberal democracy is a fragile system that can always veer into a more dangerous form of ideology (totalitarianism), but it is nonetheless the 'least bad' option. This position seems defensible enough on its own, though Žižek grows increasingly sceptical about it on the practical level over the course of this period. The problem on the level of theory, however, is that he cannot effectively translate liberal democracy as a solution into his reading of Lacan.

Žižek's loss of faith in democracy frees him to further develop his understanding of Lacan, especially those aspects of Lacan's thought (above all the notion of the psychoanalytic cure, as I will discuss in later chapters) that his early commitment to democracy did not allow him to integrate fully into his overall theory. Only after this shift toward what I am here calling his 'middle' period does theology begin to play a central role in Žižek's work. The goal of this chapter, then, is ultimately to show how he arrived at the impasse that made the shift necessary. In order to explain Žižek's theory of ideology, I will first need to summarize the theory to which he is responding – that of the French Marxist Louis Althusser. I will then explain what Žižek's use of Lacan adds to this theory. My focus will be on three crucial concepts that remain central at every stage of Žižek's work: the big Other, the Real and *jouissance* (or enjoyment). With these concepts in hand, I will conclude by showing how Žižek applies them in his analysis of liberalism, racism and nationalism.⁵ My focus, therefore, will be on the first and third aspects of Žižek's project – an exposition of Lacan and the development of a Lacanian theory of ideology critique. I will deal with Hegel at certain points, but for the most part, Žižek's reading of Hegel and of German Idealism more generally will be held in reserve for the next chapter.

Ideology in practice

Sublime Object begins with a reference to the debate between Jürgen Habermas and Michel Foucault, which Žižek characterizes as 'the great debate occupying the foreground of today's [i.e., the late 1980s] intellectual scene'. At the risk of oversimplifying, this debate could be seen as a confrontation between a classical Enlightenment position with its emphasis on uncoerced deliberation among reasonable subjects (Habermas) and a 'postmodern' position that emphasizes the all-pervasive role of power in shaping societies and individuals (Foucault). Žižek notes that Habermas's primary contribution to this debate, *The Philosophical Discourse of Modernity* (1985), only mentions Lacan in passing and does not mention Althusser at all, leading him to claim that the conflict between Habermas and Foucault 'is masking another opposition, another debate which is theoretically more far-reaching: the Althusser–Lacan debate'. Habermas's lack of specific attention to Lacan and total silence on Althusser is a prominent example of a broader tendency: Lacan is viewed as simply one among many French 'postmodernist' thinkers (a view that Žižek completely rejects), and Althusser seems to have been forgotten altogether.[6] In the pages that follow, Lacan turns out (as always) to have the superior theory, but here Žižek gives the impression that no one can truly understand Lacan's importance without first understanding Althusser.[7]

In terms of intellectual history, this has a certain plausibility. One of the most prominent French thinkers of the postwar period, Althusser was closely connected to Lacan in many ways. He wrote a major essay on Lacan[8] and frequently used concepts from Lacanian psychoanalysis in his work. Beyond that, he gave his student Jacques-Alain Miller the fateful advice to 'read all of Lacan', which Miller actually did – an initial step down the path that would lead Miller to marry Lacan's daughter, edit his seminars for publication, and ultimately serve as Lacan's chief interpreter and intellectual heir. But the importance of Althusser for Zizek's work is also rooted in his own experience in Yugoslavia. As he tells us in *Tarrying with the Negative*, Žižek observed how all the conflicting academic schools of thought in Yugoslavia seemed to be able to agree on one thing: Althusser was no good. For Žižek, this was an important clue – the universal disavowal of Althusser served as an unwitting admission that Althusser was dangerous because his work revealed all too clearly the way the Yugoslav Communists maintained their hold on power.[9] Clearly, then, Althusser's theory of ideology is not important simply as a stepping stone to Lacan. For Žižek, it has considerable value in itself.

Althusser's main contribution to the theory of ideology is his essay 'Ideology and Ideological State Apparatuses'.[10] In this essay, he is trying to develop a theory of how a particular economic system or mode of production manages to perpetuate or reproduce itself over time. In order for this to occur, a lot more is necessary than generating a profit here and now – the system must also make sure that fresh workers are continually being trained, that capitalists have ways of enforcing their property claims, and so on. In order to explain the continual reproduction of a mode of production, Althusser says that Marxists need to shift their emphasis. In traditional Marxism, a given society is conceived as having a base, which encompasses the economic realm, and a superstructure, which is divided into two levels: the state and ideology. Althusser agrees with the notion, first formulated by Engels, that the base determines the superstructure 'in the last instance' – that is to say, everything is ultimately explainable in economic terms. He believes, however, that Marxist theorists have tended to overemphasize the 'last instance' and so to ignore the fact that the superstructure has a 'relative autonomy' and can exercise a 'reciprocal action' on the base.[11]

In the case of the state, it is fairly obvious how the superstructure can act on the base: by forcibly closing factories, for instance, or by breaking a strike. In order to demonstrate how ideology can exert this 'reciprocal action', Althusser must broaden the understanding of ideology. Generally, ideology is understood first of all as a set of (false) beliefs. The task of traditional ideology critique is to point out how the dominant ideology actually serves as misleading propaganda for the capitalist system. So for instance, one might argue that the bourgeois notion of 'freedom' really amounts to the freedom of the capitalist to exploit the worker, or something along those lines. Althusser recognizes the truth in this form of ideology critique, but doesn't think it goes far enough. One must view the ideas themselves as a secondary phenomenon and turn one's attention to the concrete institutions and practices that produce them, such as schools, churches and family structures. Althusser calls these institutions 'Ideological State Apparatuses', and they serve as a kind of persuasion or 'soft power' alongside the coercive force of the repressive 'state power' (the police or the army). These two sides of the superstructure work together to ensure the continued existence of the dominant mode of production.

To illustrate how Ideological State Apparatuses work, Althusser draws on a famous argument from Pascal, which Žižek also quotes in *Sublime Object*.[12] If someone is struggling to believe, Pascal recommends simply acting like a Christian (going to mass, kneeling down to pray) – belief will follow soon enough. This is obviously a reversal of our normal conception, where our actions are ideally supposed to be guided by our beliefs, but at the same time, it reflects everyday experience. For instance, one will often find idealistic young people who for one reason or another feel they need to take mainstream corporate jobs, even though it contradicts their stated beliefs. Over time, these radicals will begin to espouse more 'realistic' views – their day-to-day practices at work don't simply contradict, but will ultimately *change* their beliefs. Similarly, 'mega churches' in the United States such as Willow Creek, which use popular music, live drama and other enticements to attract people who might otherwise find church boring, rely (consciously or unconsciously) on Pascal's insight. Their success reflects the fact that simply by virtue of doing the bare minimum of consistently showing up for church on Sunday, even for a church service that is basically free of traditional Christian practices, people will come to identify as Christians. On the flip side, one finds a similar approach among Christians (mainly those who are theologically educated) who believe it is crucial for churches to either reintroduce or reinvigorate traditional liturgical practices. For them, Christianity has been emptied of its distinctiveness – the solution, however, is not to teach people theology directly, but to change their practices.

It is clear, then, that the material basis of ideology (in the sense of beliefs) is not directly the economic system as such, but people's everyday habits or practices. For Althusser, the primary Ideological State Apparatus in modern society is the school, where students learn various types of 'know-how' – ranging from science and literature to job skills and norms of social interaction. This 'know-how' is basically a way to ensure submission to the dominant system, but the subjects involved experience it as a set of 'skills' that they have acquired and that they should dutifully perform.[13] Ideological beliefs then serve as a series of rationalizations, covering up the true nature of one's actions. As Althusser puts it: 'Ideology represents the imaginary relationship of individuals to their real conditions of existence.'[14] Thus, for example, one might observe that by working hard, a worker is making the owner richer and not gaining much for himself aside from exhaustion. Ideology does not tell a worker in that situation, 'Yes, the owner is only paying you enough to survive, while your labour generates much more wealth for him – nevertheless, this situation is fair because . . .' Instead, ideology says, 'Those who work hard are rewarded' or 'A strong work ethic is an important virtue.'

Although ideology is an imaginary picture of the subject's relationship to the system, Althusser believes that the majority of people never question it. They recognize their ideological beliefs as more or less obviously true, and they act in general as though living in ideology is the most natural thing in the world. This is because, for Althusser, living in ideology *is* the most natural thing in the world – paraphrasing Aristotle, he claims that 'man [*sic*] is an ideological animal by nature'.[15] Human subjects owe their existence as subjects to ideology. He understands this dependency on ideology in terms of a call or 'interpellation' – ideology, imagined as a powerful Subject (analogous to God), calls or 'interpellates' the individual subject, causing the subject to recognize himself or herself as 'subject' to the demands of ideology.[16]

There is no actual moment when the subject is actually first 'called' by ideology and no time 'before' – as Althusser says, 'ideology has always-already interpellated individuals as subjects'.[17] However, this hypothetical call is continually reenacted in everyday life. In a famous example, Althusser asks us to imagine someone walking down the street and hearing a police officer yell from behind: 'Hey, you there!' The person turns around, and '[b]y this mere one-hundred-and-eighty-degree physical conversion, he becomes a *subject*', which is to say, he shows that he recognizes ideological authority and recognizes himself as accountable to that authority.[18] Althusser emphasizes again and again how remarkable it is that the 'correct' individual (i.e., the one the police officer intended) turns around nearly every time. For him, this reliable response proves that subjects naturally acknowledge ideological authority. It is this (true) recognition of the power of ideology and of themselves as subject to it that makes it possible for ideology to cause them to *mis*recognize the real meaning of their actions.

The challenge of cynicism

As noted above, Žižek found Althusser's theory of ideology to be true to his experience in Yugoslavia. His description of precisely *how* it fit his experience, however, provides some insight into where he departs from it:

> The resistance to Althusser [among Yugoslav academics] confirmed how it was precisely the Althusserian theory – often defamed as proto-Stalinist – which served as a kind of 'spontaneous' theoretical tool for effectively undermining the Communist totalitarian regimes: his theory of the Ideological State-Apparatuses assigned the crucial role in the reproduction of an ideology to 'external' rituals and practices with regard to which 'inner' beliefs and convictions are strictly secondary. And is it necessary to call attention to the central place of such rituals in 'real socialism'? What counted in it was external obedience, not 'inner conviction.' *Obedience coincided with the semblance of obedience,* which is why the only way to be truly 'subversive' was to act 'naively' [that is, to take the ideology literally], to make the system 'eat its own words,' i.e., to undermine the *appearance* of its ideological consistency.[19]

Up to the final sentence, this quotation seems to correspond fairly closely with Althusser's theory. The twist comes at the end – Althusser never says that acting 'naively' will undermine the system. In his theory, basically everyone (with the exception of criminals) acts 'naively'. Thus in Yugoslavia, Žižek found himself living in a situation that Althusser does not seem to have anticipated, one where virtually everyone knows that the official ideology is a lie, where almost no one consciously 'believed in it', and yet where this near-universal cynicism had no effect on the ruling system's power. How could this be?

To understand this strange phenomenon, Žižek works within the basic terms of Althusser's theory, but radicalizes it. Althusser was right to put the emphasis on practice in the critique of ideology, but he was still working within the traditional paradigm that equates 'ideology' with 'false (conscious) beliefs'. For Žižek, this

Ideology critique

equation of ideology with a lack of adequate knowledge 'leaves out an illusion, an error, a distortion which is already at work in the social reality itself, at the level of what the individuals are *doing*, and not only what they *think* or *know* they are doing'.[20] The example he uses in the first chapter of *Sublime Object* – an example to which we will be returning later in this chapter – is the way money functions under capitalism, as described by Marx in the opening chapters of *Capital*. Everyone consciously knows that money is 'just paper' and that it only serves as a universal equivalent because everyone has tacitly agreed to treat it as a universal equivalent. Yet everyone nonetheless *behaves* as though money directly embodied a quasi-magical quality called 'value', that is, as though it is intrinsically valuable. This isn't simply a mistake that people unwittingly find themselves making – it is an illusion that lies at the heart of the capitalist system, which is premised on the perpetual accumulation of more and more money for its own sake.[21]

This argument brings together two moves that will return again and again throughout Žižek's work. The first is a general principle that he takes from Hegel: what seems to be an obstacle on the level of knowledge is actually an obstacle in the object of knowledge itself (or, in technical philosophical terms, what seems to be an epistemological obstacle is an ontological fault). In this case, on the first approach it appears that the problem is that people hold distorted, 'ideological' beliefs – but the real problem is that the underlying social reality itself is distorted. The second principle is perhaps more dispositional than strictly philosophical – Žižek is very loyal to his sources and is therefore disdainful of thinkers who rush to change their concepts in changed situations. In this case, the advent of the culture of cynicism, which was certainly not limited to Yugoslavia, has led many leftist intellectuals to believe that the concept of ideology has outlived its usefulness. This position is not entirely unreasonable: if everyone knows that the ideas that legitimate the system are false but nonetheless continue to go along with the system, it seems foolish to expose the ideas that legitimate the system as false and expect results (after all, everyone already knows). Žižek, however, believes this rejection of the concept of ideology is overhasty. Though it is correct that traditional ideology critique is no longer possible, the culture of cynicism actually helps us to see *more clearly* how ideology always functioned.

Specifically, it allows us to see that ideology *always* includes some degree of cynical distance. Subjects never fully identify with ideology: there is always some non-interpellated 'leftover'.[22] Thus, though the basic structure of Althusser's theory of ideology remains in place, his notion of interpellation as a straightforward operation whereby ideology, as it were, swallows the subject whole must undergo some serious changes. This is where Lacanian psychoanalysis comes in.

Ideology and the big Other

At this point, an obvious question arises: if people know that the system is based on lies, then why do they go along with it? In the commonsense view, this is the level where it seems most natural to turn to psychoanalysis, the level of the individual psyche. Even if one is sceptical of the value of psychoanalysis, it is more or less clear that this is the kind of problem psychoanalysis deals with. Seemingly more problematic is the other, equally obvious question: what does it mean for social reality to have an internal obstacle? Here the reference to psychoanalysis seems more problematic, and perhaps even illegitimate. It may somehow be possible to 'apply' the insights of psychoanalysis to the social level, but many would argue – and have argued – that this would depend on a false analogy between society as a whole and the individual psyche. For Žižek, however, this is a false dichotomy, as well as a false view of what psychoanalysis (at least in Lacan's version) is about. Psychoanalysis doesn't deal with the individual psyche *as opposed to* the social order. Rather, it deals with the 'interface' between the two, with the ways in which the individual and the social are irreducibly related. Thus psychoanalysis does more than simply allow us to answer the first question and 'apply' those insights to answering the second – it allows us, and indeed *requires* us, to answer both questions at once.

Still, in a linear presentation, I need to start with one or the other, and so I will start with the social level.[23] As noted above, in Althusser's theory, the domain of ideology lies in the various institutions in which we move. Althusser lists several examples, with the proviso that he is relying on our intuitive sense of what

Ideology critique

an institution is and that further work needs to be determine these institutions' nature on a rigorous theoretical level.[24] All of his examples are basically 'brick and mortar' institutions like churches, schools, political parties and so on. In order to bring this idea of institutions into contact with Lacanian theory, Žižek implicitly expands the reach of what counts as an institution to include anything in social life that the subject experiences as existing independently of any particular individual – for instance, non-codified social norms, recognized social rituals like handshaking,[25] and language itself.

Taken together, these official and quasi-official 'institutions' constitute what Lacan calls the symbolic order. The fundamental model for all these various institutions is the subject's relationship to *language*. Lacan's understanding of language is couched in the terms of the school of mid-century French linguistics known as 'structuralism', but departs significantly from structuralism in many respects (for this reason, Lacan is often called a 'poststructuralist'). The key insight of structuralism is that language is a *differential* system of *signifiers*. Linguistic units – including, but not limited to, words – are signifiers in that they point away from themselves, and their interrelationships are differential in that signifiers are defined by what they are not. To take a standard example, we only know what 'b' is because it is not 'p' – 'b' as a sound has no value except insofar as we can tell it apart from all the other sounds. Therefore language is *reflexive*, meaning that language only refers to language (words refer to other words), instead of referring in some straightforward way to 'the real world'.

With this concept of language in mind, it is easy to imagine an endless chain of signifiers, each referring to the next in an infinite procession, never landing on anything. In order to bring some degree of order and stability to this signifying chain, a kind of short-circuit must intervene in the form of a 'master signifier' or 'quilting point' (*point de capiton*). The master signifier is a signifier just like any other, but instead of referring to other signifiers, it refers only to *itself*. The way this works is clearly illustrated by Marx's concept of commodity fetishism, which is discussed by Žižek in the first chapter of *Sublime Object*. Marx begins by envisioning a primitive barter system, where the value of a given commodity is thought of in terms of what other commodities it will buy (a pound of wheat for a gallon of oil, perhaps). Then he introduces money as one commodity among others – a universal equivalent, but still thought of primarily in terms of what it can buy. The final step into commodity fetishism is when this logic is reversed: money refers to value as such, and all other commodities are thought of in terms of how much money one can get for them. That is, money as a commodity becomes self-referential – money is worth (signifies) *money* instead of being worth X number of other commodities – and all other commodities are worth (signify) *money*.[26] Even though as a material object it is virtually worthless, commodity fetishism confers on money a mystical aura of intrinsic value, which is why Marx calls it 'fetishism', a term that originally referred to non-Western or 'pagan' religious practices.

Thus we can see that the master signifier is a completely empty or meaningless signifier, but it provides the illusion of a fullness of meaning that gives all other signifiers something to 'crystallize' or 'quilt' around. The sure sign of a master signifier, therefore, is that any attempt at explanation ends in a tautology. For instance, why should I obey the law? Ultimately, I should obey *because it's the law*. For Žižek as for Lacan, the name for this empty self-referentiality is 'subject'. Therefore, as Žižek explains at great length in *For They Know Not*, the self-referential master signifier is what *subjectifies* the symbolic order, that is, what makes it possible to regard the symbolic order as another subject.[27] From this subjectivization derives the Lacanian term that Žižek tends to use most in referring to the symbolic order: the big Other. Before the modern period in Europe, the ultimate big Other was none other than God – the church guided society in the name of God, the king ruled by divine right, and everyone had their proper places in the social order as allotted by God. (And why should we care how God thinks we should order society? *Because he's God!*) This analogy between God and the big Other becomes very significant in Žižek's work on Christianity, but it is important to note that in the modern period, God is no longer the privileged name for the big Other. Instead, one sees the basic structure of the big Other at work under a variety of names or at times as the unnamed but presupposed author of social rules, as when one says, 'That's just how it's done.' Even though the public space of the Western world is now for the most part secular and only a handful of conspiracy theorists believe that

Ideology critique

there really is some discrete individual 'pulling the strings', everyone still acts as though there is some Other out there – some very *big* Other – who holds together the social order.

Once again, we find here the core principle of Žižek's theory of ideology: belief in the big Other is found at the level of people's *practice*, not their knowledge. Here the psychoanalytic concept of the unconscious enters in an unexpected way. The most fundamental aspect of the unconscious is what Žižek calls 'fantasy', and it is unconscious in the most rigorous possible sense – it can never become conscious, never be fully identified with. Normally one thinks of the unconscious as some deep or hidden level of the self, but here the unconscious fantasy immediately overlaps with the social practices at the heart of ideology.[28] Those practices are also necessarily 'unconscious' in the sense that if subjects really came to *know* what they were doing, to really confront the fantasy structuring their social reality, that reality would profoundly change. Ideology represents 'the paradox of a being which can reproduce itself only insofar as it is misrecognised and overlooked: the moment we see it "as it really is", this being dissolves itself into nothingness or, more precisely, it changes into another kind of reality'.[29]

The stumbling block of the Real

As the reference to the transition from feudalism to modernity implies, no master signifier, and therefore no particular symbolic order, is permanent. The big Other does not collapse due to outside pressure, however, but due to the inherent deadlock that in Lacanian terminology is known as the Real. The concept of the Real is one of the most important concepts in Žižek's project, but it is also the most difficult to understand. This is partly because any attempt to talk about the Real 'in itself', to give a 'definition' of the term, necessarily winds up being simultaneously very abstract and bewilderingly paradoxical. Such definitions can be very helpful and clarifying after one is already familiar with the concept, but here I will try to remain as concrete as possible, at least at first. This also provides a good opportunity to illustrate the dialectical process, since Žižek says that Hegelian dialectics is the closest parallel to the logic of the Lacanian Real.[30]

As the adoption of the slogan 'members of the reality-based community' by liberals in the US shows, most people would agree that, at least ideally, our social order should be based in *reality*, not in fantasy. Even the Bush administration official who first coined the term 'reality-based community', bizarrely intending it as a slur toward liberals, would probably agree in principle – the only difference being that he thinks our social order should be based on American power, which can transform the present reality that liberals (unambitiously) regard as an unchanging point of reference.[31]

It seems clear enough that no present social order is based directly on reality. The question then becomes, why not? As the first step for this dialectic, one could present a more or less intuitive answer: some particular obstacle has kept us from doing this, but it is still possible if we try harder. Many candidates for the obstacle present themselves. Perhaps science has not yet progressed far enough. Perhaps science *has* progressed far enough, but religious ideology keeps us from acting on what science teaches us. Or perhaps human greed and lust for power more generally have stood in the way, but by becoming enlightened, we can overcome those negative forces. Thinking along these lines, fairly soon one comes up against obstacles that seem to be irreducible – that is, an inherent part of human nature. So as a second step, one could then say: no, it's not just some contingent obstacle that we can get rid of. Basing society directly on extra-social reality is simply impossible. We can continually approximate it, but due to our human finitude, we must resign ourselves to never reaching the fullness of reality.

What is wrong with this second position? It seems sensible enough and is in fact held by many people in one form or another, but it is ultimately self-undermining. On the surface, it breaks clearly with the first option. Yet if one looks closely, it is clear that this position still regards 'basing society on reality' as something that *should* be possible. This is the only way that the talk of 'approximating' makes sense. It is still stuck within the frame of the first option, where some removable obstacle stands in our way, and it has simply made the obstacle so big as to be insurmountable. Thus the third and final step of the dialectic is to change the frame itself: yes, it is inherently impossible to base our society on reality, and the obstacle is inherent to reality itself. One could summarize this procedure as follows:

Ideology critique

1. Basing our society on reality is possible, and we haven't done so because of some removable obstacle.
2. No, it's impossible, and isn't that a shame?
3. No, *it's impossible* – and in fact, reality is what's tripping us up.

This final step amounts to a shift from the concept of 'reality' to the concept of the Real. The frame of the first two positions, within which basing society on reality seems to be possible in principle, is ultimately the idea of reality as a smooth, harmonious, internally consistent thing. The third step reveals that this 'naïve' or commonsense understanding of 'reality' must be discarded in favour of the Lacanian notion of the Real. As Žižek will say again and again, the Real is as far as possible from an underlying harmony – it is a fundamental antagonism, a deadlock, a contradiction, an unbearable tension.

The many paradoxical 'definitions' of the Real, often quite reminiscent of the contradictory ways of designating God in Pseudo-Dionysius's *Divine Names*, are so many ways to try to get at the idea of a fundamental self-contradiction at the very heart of existence. The contradictory nature of the Real's relationship to the symbolic order is perhaps the most revealing 'definition' in this context. On the one hand, the Real represents the evasive remainder that the symbolic order can never 'catch' and contain in its attempt to ground the social reality in the Real – it's what the symbolic somehow never manages to reach. On the other hand, the Real is the fundamental contradiction at the heart of the symbolic order, actively undermining it – the problem is not that we can't reach it, but that it's all too close. The ideological fantasy that underlies our social reality is a necessarily failed attempt simultaneously to contain and to evade the traumatic antagonism of the Real.

Thus we can see that we are far from the traditional view of ideology as incorrect knowledge: 'in the Lacanian perspective ideology rather designates *a totality set on effacing the traces of its own impossibility*'.[32] This impossibility appears in different guises at different times and places. Under capitalism, class struggle serves as the fundamental antagonism preventing the establishment of a harmonious social order. What this means specifically is that under capitalism, all individuals are considered to be formally equal and to exchange goods and services on the basis of arrangements freely entered into. Some people, members of the working class, have nothing to sell on the market except their own labour power. Members of the capitalist class, who own factories or other means of production, are able to purchase this labour power for its fair market value or 'replacement cost' – that is, how much it costs to meet the worker's basic needs and enable him to work again the next day. In Marxist theory, however, labour is a special type of commodity in that it is the only commodity that can actually *create* value above and beyond its replacement cost. The capitalists are therefore able to generate a 'surplus value' beyond what it costs to pay a subsistence wage, and in terms of the 'free' labour contract, the worker has 'freely' surrendered any claim on this surplus value. Thus in practice, the system that treats every person as formally equally to all other persons winds up producing two separate classes of people, one class amassing more and more wealth from others' labour, over against the class of people who must sell their labour power in order to survive. Getting the working class to go along with this arrangement is a difficult task, and when the capitalists have failed to do so, it has resulted in violent confrontations and in some cases even full-blown revolutions.

In Althusser's terms, then, the superstructure of ideology is not only necessary to continue to reproduce the base of the economic system, but also serves to attempt to prevent the self-contradictions of the system from exploding and bringing down the entire social structure. The Real as antagonism, however, is not reducible to any of its historical forms: 'The kernel of the Real encircled by failed attempts to symbolize-totalize it is radically *non-historical*: history itself is nothing but a succession of failed attempts to grasp, conceive, specify this strange kernel.'[33]

Keeping enjoyment at bay

In the course of answering the question of what it means for the social order to have an inherent obstacle, another question has likely arisen in many readers' minds: If the attempt to establish a social totality always fails, why bother trying? With this question in the air, it seems that the question that I initially deferred – why do cynical subjects still go along with the system? – has only become more difficult to answer. Once again, however, the questions on the social level and the individual level must be answered together, and in this case, the answer can be summed up in one word: *jouissance*. This French word can best be translated by 'enjoyment', and its meaning overlaps both with the straightforward sense of 'enjoyment' and the idea of 'enjoyment' in terms of having the 'enjoyment' (free use) of another person's property or 'enjoying' certain rights. However, its connotations are more intense and more specifically sexual than the English 'enjoyment', because it is also the word for orgasm. For this reason, in discussions of Lacan and of many other twentieth-century French thinkers, *jouissance* is normally left in the original French. Žižek tends to alternate between '*jouissance*' and 'enjoyment', but when he uses the English term, the connotations of the French should still be understood.

As noted at the end of the last section, the Real appears differently depending on the situation. For the sake of making an initial approximation, one could say that *jouissance* is the way that the Real manifests itself at the level of the individual subject. Depending on one's disposition, the workings of the Real at the level of the social may well seem to be a very good thing: a subversive and even liberatory undermining of an oppressive system. The picture changes significantly, however, when the same effects are envisioned at the level of the individual. The paradoxical 'definition' of the Real that is most relevant here is the one that posits the Real as simultaneously an unimaginable fullness – an impossible oversaturation – and the destructive absolute void. For the subject to be given over fully to *jouissance* is tantamount to the subject's obliteration, which here does not necessarily mean physical death, but rather the complete destruction of the subject as a social being. One can thus think of *jouissance* as analogous to Rudolph Otto's famous definition of the holy as both *mysterium tremendum* and *mysterium fascinans* – simultaneously terrifying and yet irresistibly fascinating.[34]

The ideological fantasy, which serves as the 'interface' between the individual subject and the social order, provides a means of keeping *jouissance* at a safe distance. In exchange for renouncing access to the fullness of *jouissance*, the subject is 'interpellated' or brought under the symbolic order, which opens up the space of desire. Here the same fundamental contradictions that were found at the social level repeat themselves on the individual level. Most importantly, a complete and total 'interpellation' – such as Althusser seems to envision in his theory of ideology – is by definition impossible. The attempt to extract the subject from the fullness of *jouissance* always necessarily results in a 'leftover', a tiny bit of *jouissance*. The Lacanian name for this leftover is *objet petit a* ('object little a'), or simply *objet a*. A full explanation of how Lacan arrived at this particular name for this concept would take me much too far afield, but the basic terms are not difficult to explain. First, it is an object because the subject experiences it as foreign, as outside of himself or herself. The 'a' stands for the French *Autre*, meaning 'other', and it is 'little' because it is the leftover that results from the imposition of the big Other (*grand Autre*).

Another name for *objet petit a* is the 'object-cause of desire'. It is the *object* of desire in the sense of being the *goal* that the subject continually pursues, but never reaches. Every time the subject finally reaches some particular object of desire, therefore, it feels like a disappointment – no matter how satisfying, it is somehow still not *it*, that is, not *objet petit a*. Of course, the very nature of desire is that once desire is fulfilled, it disappears; in order to continue to exist as desire, therefore, it must remain perpetually unsatisfied. At the same time, it is the *cause* of desire in the sense that the reason that the whole structure of desire as continual deferral, as a process of constantly striving and never reaching the goal, was set up in the first place was to keep *objet a* at a safe distance. The ideological fantasy, then, serves as a kind of strategy for keeping *jouissance*, in the form of *objet petit a*, under control to a sufficient degree to provide the subject with some relative stability. This is one of the meanings of Lacan's saying, 'Desire is always the desire of the other' – the big Other teaches me how to desire. Another meaning is closely related: I always desire the other. This is because the big Other is always associated with *objet petit a* and acquires a kind of aura of *jouissance*, as is illustrated in the fascinating charisma exuded by the king or totalitarian leader. For this reason, Žižek argues that totalitarianism shows us particularly clearly that the final support of every ideology is *jouissance*.[35]

The big Other, therefore, issues the subject a kind of ultimatum: either submit to ideology, or be consumed by *jouissance*. This follows the logic of a 'forced choice', a concept that Žižek will return to again and again in his writings: 'you have freedom to choose, but on condition that you choose the right thing'.[36] Just as in Althusser's theory of interpellation, there is never some particular moment when this decision is made. Instead, insofar as the subject exists within ideology, the subject is 'always treated *as if he had already chosen*'. At first glance, this 'forced choice' seems like simple blackmail, 'a trap by means of which totalitarian Power catches its subjects'. But Žižek emphasizes that 'there is nothing "totalitarian" about it. The subject who thinks he can avoid this paradox and really have a free choice is a *psychotic* subject, one who retains a kind of distance from the symbolic order – who is not really caught in the signifying network.'[37]

As noted above, the Real is simultaneously what the symbolic order cannot reach and the antagonism tearing it down from within. In the same way, *objet petit a* is simultaneously what the subject's desire circulates around without ever being able to reach and the disruptive element at the core of the subject's being. The ideological fantasy gives both the symbolic order and the subject's own identity only a relative and always fragile stability. The fact that the two are so inextricably linked means that the fall of a given ideology – something that is always possible – is always experienced as traumatic by those who were living under it. As someone who lived under an oppressive Communist regime and participated in its overthrow, Žižek understands this much better than most Westerners, who are able to take the stability of their social order basically for granted. Speaking of the fall of the Eastern European regimes, he says that 'the breakdown of socialism is not to be underestimated, as is usually the case when one conceives of "real socialism" as an externally imposed system which oppressed some original national life-force . . . what disintegrated in Eastern Europe was *le grand Autre* [the big Other], the ultimate guarantor of the social pact'.[38] An even better example is the situation in Iraq after the fall of Saddam Hussein. In the former Communist countries, many of the basic institutions of society remained in place, but in the wake of the US-led invasion, virtually every aspect of a shared Iraqi social body was destroyed, leaving people with nothing to fall back on except ethnic or sectarian religious identity. There now appears to be no immediate way of restoring that larger social bond. This was entirely predictable, but most mainstream figures in the US, both liberal and conservative, were convinced of the possibility of 'bringing democracy to Iraq' by means of an invasion – this stemmed directly from their naïveté about the very serious consequences of the destruction (in this case, often actual *physical destruction*) of the most essential social institutions. The toppling of the big Other is not to be undertaken lightly.

Liberal democracy and nationalism

At least in these early works, the basic structure of ideology seems to be more or less inescapable. An ideological fantasy is formed through the imposition of a master signifier, which attempts to ward off the destructive force of the antagonistic Real. Still, even if there is no possibility of a perfect (i.e., permanent) solution within this basic framework, these basic attributes can be brought together in more or less stable – or, from a pessimistic point of view, more or less destructive – ways. This means that even though it is impossible to find a 'non-ideological' standpoint, it still makes sense to have preferences for particular options within the ideological field. In *Sublime Object*, Žižek's preference is clear: liberal democracy. He offers several reasons for this, perhaps the most interesting being that in elections, the democratic society formally enacts its own dissolution, such that – in a formulation he is surely embarrassed about now – elections represent an 'irruption of the Real'.[39] The embarrassment here is twofold. On the one hand, Žižek has stated many times that he finds his early enthusiasm for democracy to have been naïve, for reasons that will be discussed later in this section. On the other hand, the idea of elections as the Real does not work on the theoretical level – it treats an 'irruption of the Real' as something that can be scheduled and controlled.

Žižek's primary reason, however, is that in liberal democracy, the place of power is always left formally empty – that is, no one has an inherent right to rule, no one serves directly as the 'instrument of the big Other'.[40] Ideally at least, in a democracy, the political ruler always leads *in the name of* the people, whereas in a totalitarian system, the ruler *defines* the people. One can draw a parallel here with the logic of commodity fetishism. In a totalitarian system, the leader is like money, which directly embodies value, or put differently, puts off an 'aura' of value. Just as the value of all other commodities is defined by reference to money as the inherently valuable commodity, so also the 'people' under a totalitarian regime is defined by their loyalty to the leader – to fail to be loyal to the leader is simply to fail to be a part of 'the people'.

As I said above, Žižek identifies the 'aura' of the totalitarian ruler with *objet petit a*, the fascinating and destructive bit of *jouissance* that ties us to the ideological fantasy. Liberal democracy, by keeping this role of leader or master signifier formally empty and delegating it to particular people for a more or less limited time, tries to prevent the *jouissance* at the root of ideology from adhering to any one person. This principle is most vividly illustrated by the procedure of the Jacobins in the wake of the French Revolution, an example that Žižek returns to again and again at every stage of his work. When the Jacobins executed the king of France, they did not do so because of any specific crime he had committed – his crime was simply the fact of being an absolute monarch. The totalitarian move would have been to say, 'The king was illegitimate – *we*, however, are the rightful rulers.' Instead, they recognized that by occupying the place of power, they became just as guilty as the king was and that therefore, 'it was only a matter of time before the guillotine would cut off their heads'.[41] Since the French Revolution, no countries seem to have implemented a policy of summary execution of all leaders upon leaving office, but the same basic idea is at work in the expectation that political leaders will voluntarily relinquish power when election results or term limits require it, even if doing so means handing power over to their political enemies.

This presentation of liberal democracy seems relatively straightforward and basically matches the mainstream of contemporary political thought in the West. The problem is that it does not make sense in terms of Žižek's theory of ideology. Žižek seems to be claiming that under liberal democracy, there is no master signifier – the place where a master signifier would be is kept empty. Yet if there is no master signifier, no big Other, then it should follow that there would be mass chaos, which is not the case in most Western democracies. Already in *For They Know Not*, Žižek implicitly recognizes that this is a problem. He continues to advocate democracy, and in fact emphasizes again and again the compatibility of Hegel's philosophy with democracy (in contrast to the prevalent view that it encourages totalitarianism). The type of democracy that he describes here, however, is Hegel's vision of a constitutional monarchy. Under such a system, the king occupies the place of power, but purely as a formality – instead of directly ruling, the monarch formally endorses the policies decided upon by elected government officials and expert bureaucrats. Thus the king occupies the place of power solely *so that no one else will*. This does not deprive the king of the 'aura' that attaches to the totalitarian leader, but the king's lack of effective power keeps the inevitable totalitarian tendency of ideology relatively under control. Although it is admittedly fanciful – after all, how would one go about establishing a monarchy in a country that didn't already have one? – the fact that constitutional monarchy serves as the emblematic form of democracy in *For They Know Not* underscores the need to incorporate some kind of master signifier if democracy is to make sense within Žižek's Lacanian terms.

What the idea of constitutional monarchy does not adequately address, however, is the reason *why* master signifiers are installed in the first place: to counteract the Real of antagonism at the heart of the social body. Specifically, in the modern period during which liberal democracy arises, the fundamental social antagonism is the class struggle that is at the heart of capitalism. Žižek's illustration of the master signifier or *point de capiton* that serves to pacify this conflict is the figure of the Jew in anti-Semitism.[42] Indeed, anti-Semitism serves as Žižek's privileged example of ideology in general, and it serves as a nearly perfect illustration of his theory. In the first place, anti-Semitism shows very clearly that ideology has to do with more than merely incorrect knowledge. To argue with an anti-Semite about whether Jews are really involved in a vast conspiracy to rule the world, whether they really run every financial institution and media outlet, etc., is to miss the point. Although certain historical factors made it easy to single out the Jews rather than some other group, at bottom anti-Semitism has nothing to do with real Jews at all. This can be clearly seen in the response of anti-Semites who are asked to account for their Jewish neighbour who is a normal, decent person: the anti-Semite is able to respond, for example, that the reason this Jew appears to be good is because the Jews are so deceptive by nature. For Žižek, ideology is at its most effective when contradictions cease to register as contradictions any more[43] – as in the United States, where according to popular stereotypes, Mexicans are somehow simultaneously incredibly lazy people and also workaholics who are stealing American jobs. In *Tarrying with the Negative*, Žižek specifies how anti-Semitism fulfils the second major claim of his theory of ideology, namely that ideology is founded in *jouissance*. For Žižek, national or ethnic communities (what he here calls the 'national Thing') are ways of organizing the community's *jouissance*. When these communities' *jouissance* is disrupted by the antagonistic workings of capitalism, they respond by setting up a figure of some Other, such as the 'Jew', who is supposedly stealing their *jouissance*.[44]

The idea of the 'Jew' as master signifier may seem paradoxical, given that every example of a master signifier thus far — God, money, king, leader — has been perceived as 'positive' within the terms of ideology. Žižek makes sense of this apparent discrepancy by bringing together his analysis of liberalism and his theory of anti-Semitism. By its very nature, capitalism is anxiety-producing, continually generating new desires. In traditional societies, some master intervened in order to keep the society's fundamental antagonism from exploding, but in the modern period, the figure of the master has been toppled — that is, the space of power is left empty — and capitalism is able to run rampant. In this situation, people turn toward the national identities that are 'left over' from previous historical eras, often creating distinguished national heritages out of whole cloth. What Žižek calls the 'national Thing' becomes a way to structure the community's enjoyment by establishing a stable way of life. The conflictual nature of capitalism prevents this stability from being established, however, and so the 'national Thing' (for instance, 'America') necessarily generates the figure of the racial Other (for instance, 'illegal immigrants') who is stealing our *jouissance*. In the extreme case, fascism can arise, as a new master presents himself as the true protector of the 'national Thing'. The task then becomes to purge the Other from the social body in order to 'restore' the mythical lost harmony.[45] The most extreme and terrifying version of this 'logic' is of course Nazism.

For Žižek, the least liberals can do is to oppose this phenomenon with a more cosmopolitan vision, but in fact, Western liberals increasingly regard racist outbursts as somehow 'understandable'. Žižek sees this tacit sympathy for nationalism as deeply insidious: 'This shift in the zeitgeist is where the real danger lurks:

it prepares the ground for the possible hegemony of an ideology which perceives the presence of "aliens" as a threat to national identity, as the principal cause of antagonisms that divide the political body.' Liberals who express these attitudes are displaying a new, 'postmodern' form of racism – instead of being directly racist in the traditional sense, they take it for granted that of course 'others' ('rednecks', Eastern Europeans, people in the Third World) are naturally racist. A deeply racist attitude is paradoxically expressed in terms of opposition to racism.[46]

Describing the fall of the big Other in Eastern Europe, Žižek says that 'suddenly the spell was broken, "nothing was the same as before", reasons which a moment ago were perceived as reasons *for* ... now function as reasons *against*'.[47] If that is the case, then Žižek's analysis of nationalism in *Tarrying* represents the definitive fall of liberal democracy as his 'big Other'. The very feature that Žižek initially saw as liberalism's saving grace, the empty place of power, now becomes the structure that opens the space for the rise of racist nationalism. In later works, Žižek will analyse the phenomenon of fascism at greater length, but in *Tarrying*, the prime focus is on the failings of liberalism – including scathing critiques of Western liberals' romanticization of Eastern Europe's discovery of democracy and of the phenomenon of political correctness. In many respects, these critiques sound like right-wing polemic, but the motivation is profoundly different. Right-wing figures tend to criticize liberals as insufficiently nationalistic, sometimes even as outright traitors to their country. Žižek attacks liberalism because he had initially hoped that it could provide a defence against nationalism – instead he found that it directly *generated* nationalist movements.

Despite his revulsion at the rise of nationalism, however, Žižek never renounces – in fact, never even *critiques* – the movements that brought down Real Socialism, a process in which he participated. They may have ended up being nothing but 'vanishing mediators' between Communism and nationalism,[48] but *as 'vanishing mediators'*, they were nevertheless participating in something authentic, something that was unambiguously 'worth it', and indeed, something '*stricto sensu non-ideological*'.[49] The middle phase of Žižek's work, to which the next chapter is devoted, is an extended attempt to grapple with the concept of the 'vanishing mediator' – not initially through political analysis, but at the level of theory.

Chapter 2
Subjectivity and ethics

Tarrying with the Negative serves as a kind of 'hinge' between the early and middle stages. As discussed at the end of the previous chapter, it accomplishes the negative gesture of a break with liberalism. Though this break appears to have been prompted most directly by events in Eastern Europe, I have argued that, in retrospect, one can see that adherence to liberal democracy did not fit within his conceptual scheme. This fall of the 'big Other' of liberalism does not lead directly to the choice of some other particular political scheme, not even the Leninism that his later work is often thought to 'advocate'. Instead, it drives Žižek to deepen and expand his theory. This 'retreat into theory' is ultimately what brings Žižek to the place where an engagement with Christian theology will become not only a possibility, but an urgent task. The next chapter will cover his three books on Christianity from the early 2000s and related material from *The Ticklish Subject* (1999), while the current chapter deals with his development leading up to that point, focusing primarily on *Tarrying with the Negative* (1993), *The Indivisible Remainder* (1996) and *The Plague of Fantasies* (1997).

In addition to accomplishing the break with liberalism, *Tarrying* begins the trajectory that will drive Žižek's theoretical development throughout these works: deepening his account of subjectivity by more closely connecting Lacan with the full heritage of German Idealism. Already in *Sublime Object*, bringing together Lacan and Hegel was a major part of Žižek's stated project. In practice, the 'Lacanian reading of Hegel', as carried out in *Sublime Object* and especially in *For They Know Not*, consisted of drawing parallels between the two thinkers' major concepts – for instance, between the Hegelian dialectic and the Lacanian concept of the Real, as seen in the previous chapter. The extended readings of Kant in *Tarrying* and of Schelling in *Indivisible Remainder*, focusing particularly on the theory of subjectivity, can be seen as an expansion of the 'Lacanian reading of Hegel' into a more general 'philosophical reading of Lacan'. All along, Žižek has implicitly been reading Lacan as a philosopher, that is, treating his reformulation of psychoanalysis as a system of speculative philosophy, largely abstracted from its original context in psychoanalytic practice. In this stage, Žižek takes the next step of explicitly making a case for treating Lacan as a true philosopher in the tradition of German Idealism and of clarifying precisely what he wants from Lacan – including, perhaps most importantly, the idea of the subject as 'vanishing mediator'.

As illustrated by Žižek's extended defence of the notion of subjectivity against some of the most influential schools of European philosophy and its American heirs in *The Ticklish Subject*, the notion of the subject takes a leading role in the works treated in this chapter. This does not take place in isolation from the other aspects of his project, however, but rather spurs further development in all areas. For instance, Žižek clarifies his understanding of the Real and its relationship to ideology in ways that make it possible to answer a question that is still outstanding from the previous chapter: why is it subversive to take ideology literally? More generally, he expands on his contention in *Sublime Object* that every stance on subjectivity implies an ethics.[1] In terms of his later turn to theology, Žižek's most important move on this front is to more thoroughly integrate a major part of Lacanian theory that, while already present in *Sublime Object*, most often seemed like a foreign body in his project: the so-called psychoanalytic cure. In light of Žižek's advocacy of democracy as a 'least bad' option, Lacan's late teachings on the cure appeared to be tantamount to sheer nihilism. Žižek's break with democracy frees him not only to embrace the notion of the cure, but to claim, paradoxically, that the seemingly nihilistic cure represents a particularly radical form of *ethics*.

As will become clear in the next chapter, all of these developments provide the backdrop for Žižek's reading of Christianity. In order to situate the turn to theology, however, it is important to understand all these concepts not as what Žižek happened to be working with when he happened to turn to theology, but rather as part of the trajectory that ultimately drives him to theology. In the wake of the rejection of liberal democracy as the final horizon, Žižek does not simply turn toward a kind of scholasticism of Lacan, endlessly spinning his wheels developing ever more complex accounts of the relationship among the subject, the big Other and the Real. Instead, the ultimate goal of his theoretical development is to discover the possibility of a *new* politics. This means that ideology critique – understood as unmasking how ideology really operates, whether in its traditional or Lacanian forms – must ultimately become more than mere ideology critique.

In *Tarrying*, he takes a crucial step in this direction: 'The truly radical critique of ideology should therefore go beyond the self-congratulatory "social analyses" which continue to participate in the fantasy that sustains the object of their critique and to search for ways to sap the force of this underlying fantasy-frame itself.'[2] By the time he comes to write *Indivisible Remainder* – a book founded on a reading of speculative theological texts of Schelling – he is prepared to go even further. The link between ideology and enjoyment does not mean

> that there is no escape, that every subversion of the existing power structure is false, illusory, caught in advance in the network of what it endeavors to undermine, but the exact opposite: [. . .] the foundations of Power can be shaken because the very stability of its mighty edifice hinges on an inconsistent, fragile balance. The other conclusion to be drawn is deeply solidary with the preceding one, although it may give rise to the false impression of contradicting it: perhaps the moment has come to leave behind the old Leftist obsession with ways and means to 'subvert' or 'undermine' the Order, and to focus on the opposite question [. . .]: not how can we undermine the existing order, but *how does an Order emerge out of disorder in the first place?*[3]

At this point in his work, Žižek still seems to be largely caught in the paradigm of a revolution as 'vanishing mediator' between two forms of ideology, with the resultant form hopefully (but not always) turning out somehow better than the one it replaces. The crucial step toward the possibility of a qualitatively different form of sociality comes, as we will see in the next chapter, out of

Žižek's encounter with Alain Badiou in *The Ticklish Subject* – and Žižek's subsequent attempt to demonstrate that psychoanalysis can 'provide the foundation of a new political practice'[4] takes the form of a series of attempts to account for what is distinctive in the emergence of Christianity.

This chapter will at once trace the trajectory that leads Žižek to his encounter with theology and focus on the concepts that are most important for understanding the terms of that encounter. I will begin with his clarification of the concept of the Real in terms of Lacan's notion of 'sexual difference', then turn to the role of the subject as 'vanishing mediator' in the foundation of the symbolic order. I will conclude by discussing Žižek's philosophical – and specifically ethical – reading of the psychoanalytic diagnostic categories and Lacan's later notion of the cure.

The Real as sexual difference

The previous chapter laid out the notion of the Real as a fundamental antagonism that, roughly speaking, appears differently in different situations: as *jouissance* at the level of the individual subject, as class struggle at the level of capitalist society. For Lacan, the most fundamental contradiction is sexual difference, and all other manifestations of the Real can be understood as variations on this ultimate deadlock. Understandably, this is one of Lacan's most controversial teachings, particularly among feminists, some of whom view it as effectively saying that patriarchy is written into the very essence of human society and is therefore inescapable.[5] The natural approach in a philosophical reading of Lacan would thus seem to mean downplaying 'sexual difference' as a mere metaphor and explaining the concept of the Real in less inflammatory terms, particularly since Žižek takes the antagonism of the Real to extend to every level of existence, not only human society. Primarily out of loyalty to Lacan, however, and perhaps also out of an unadmirable desire to annoy feminists, Žižek does not take this route. Instead, he insists on retaining the sexual language – and in fact, he reads Lacan's account of sexual difference in terms of Kant and in turn claims that Kant discovered 'sexual difference'. To understand the basic conceptual shape of what

Subjectivity and ethics

Žižek is getting at here without getting bogged down in his gendered language, it seems best to start with Kant.

In *Tarrying with the Negative*, Žižek argues that Descartes covered over the true importance of his own discovery of self-consciousness through the famous formula 'I think, therefore I am [*cogito ergo sum*].' Later generations remember Descartes as the one who proved the existence of the subject as 'thinking thing [*res cogitans*]', but for Žižek, this is a secondary move that covers over his real discovery: the subject as pure void, with no place in the existing order of things. Among Descartes' successors, 'Only Kant fully articulates the inherent paradoxes of self-consciousness' in the proper sense of the empty *cogito*.[6] All three of Kant's critiques – the *Critique of Pure Reason* (on epistemology), *Critique of Practical Reason* (on ethics), and *Critique of Judgment* (on aesthetics) – display these 'inherent paradoxes', but for Žižek, the underlying logic of the paradoxes is most clearly displayed in the 'antinomies of pure reason' found in the first critique. There Kant posits four antinomies or contradictions that the (necessary) categories of pure reason inevitably generate. Using terminology derived from the third critique, Žižek divides the antinomies into two types: mathematical and dynamical.

As Žižek explains, 'mathematical antinomies arise when categories are applied to the universe as a Whole (the totality of phenomena which is never given to our finite intuition), whereas dynamical antinomies emerge when we apply categories to objects which do not belong to the phenomenal order at all (God, soul)'.[7] In the case of the dynamical antinomies, Kant asks two questions: first, whether freedom exists as a way of interrupting the flow of natural causality or whether freedom is just an illusion; and second, whether a necessary being (i.e., God) exists or not.[8] Kant argues both sides of each argument, and demonstrates that both can be proven to be true – thus one can say that the dynamical antinomies end in a *contradiction*. In the case of the mathematical antinomies, Kant again asks two questions: first, whether the universe is finite or infinite; second, whether or not all the objects we perceive can be reduced to simple parts (i.e., if there is some 'bottom level' material or materials out of which everything in the universe is made). In this case, Kant demonstrates that both sides of the argument are false. This may also seem to be a contradiction, but instead points toward the *impossibility* of conceiving of reality as a whole.

Žižek argues that Lacan's 'formulae of sexuation' expose the underlying logic of the two kinds of antinomies. The formulae themselves are presented in *Tarrying* (and in other books) with the rather confusing symbols that Lacan originally used.[9] Rather than reproduce them here, I will provide a 'translation' that corresponds with Lacan's original grid format:

Masculine Side	*Feminine Side*
There exists some X who is not submitted to the master signifier.	There does not exist any X who is exempt from the master signifier.
All X are submitted to the master signifier.	Not-all X are submitted to the master signifier.

At first glance, it appears that the formulae that are diagonal from each other are saying essentially the same thing. After all, doesn't 'All X are submitted to the master signifier' directly imply that 'There does not exist any X who is exempt from the master signifier'? And doesn't 'There exists some X who is not submitted to the master signifier' obviously mean that 'Not-all X are submitted to the master signifier'? For Žižek, however, viewing the diagonals as equivalent to each other is the greatest possible misunderstanding of these formulae – instead, one must read the vertical columns as implying each other.

On the masculine side, the logic is identical to that of the imposition of a master signifier in order to establish an ideological order, which I explained in the previous chapter. All commodities are 'submitted' to money and find their value only in relation to money – except money itself, which is inherently valuable. The only way to establish a universal realm of exchangeable commodities is to set up the commodity 'money' as an exception to the rule that commodities find their value only through exchange. More generally: not only does every universal rule necessarily imply an exception, but the exception directly constitutes the universal *as* a universal. Thus the masculine side can be summarized as the logic of the *constitutive exception*. This corresponds to

Subjectivity and ethics

the dynamical antinomies, which attempt to apply the universal categories of reason to entities outside the realm of appearances, God and free will – both of which in their own way are taken to found that realm (God by being the necessary being that provides the foundation for all others, free will by providing an absolute starting point for some chain of causality).

For the feminine side, everything hangs on the hyphen in 'not-all'. Read without the hyphen, one might think that it duplicates the masculine logic of the constitutive exception – the universal sway of a rule necessarily implies that 'not all X' is submitted to the rule, in the sense that there is some 'X' that escapes the rule. The hyphen of 'not-all', however, is meant to indicate that in the absence of an exception, the underlying X shows itself to be *inherently* incomplete or non-totalized. For this reason, Žižek defines the feminine logic as that of the *non-all*. This corresponds to the mathematical antinomies, which try to grasp the entire realm of appearances directly, without positing some exception (such as God or free will): 'although there is no object given to us in intuition which does not belong to the phenomenal field [i.e., the field of what appears to the senses], this field is never "all", never complete'.[10] Although Žižek consistently uses the term 'non-all', it is therefore helpful to note that Lacan's French phrase, *pas-tout*, can also be translated as 'non-whole'.

These two logics – the masculine logic of the *constitutive exception* and the feminine logic of the *non-all* – are not symmetrical opposites. Instead, the feminine has priority. This is because the feminine reflects the logic of the Real. Using the example from the last chapter, the subject can never gain access to the fullness of *jouissance*, yet the subject can also never escape *jouissance*. Similarly, society can never fully correspond to or overtake the Real, yet the Real is operative everywhere in society, undermining and distorting it. In short, the Real is inherently *non-all*. The masculine logic of the constitutive exception is secondary, representing what happens when one attempts to establish a smooth, harmonious, universal order: the resulting universal is necessarily contradictory or 'cracked'. This is particularly clear in the case of the master signifier – where the contradiction is that of an empty signifier representing an absolute fullness – but it extends to every area of ideology, as shown by the last chapter's example of American stereotypes that portray Mexican immigrants as lazy workaholics. Thus Lacan's 'formulae of sexuation' provide Žižek with a way of more rigorously bringing together his concepts of the ideological big Other and the Real.

At this point, Žižek may appear to be making a leap in logic. After all, in his 'mathematical' antinomies, Kant is simply saying that our attempts to grasp reality as a whole necessarily fail, whereas Žižek is saying that the Real itself is *inherently* non-all. This apparent contradiction provides a good – indeed, arguably the best possible – opportunity to discuss Žižek's reading of the relationship between Kant and Hegel. In the standard reading, Kant's philosophy opens up an irreducible gap separating the subject from the thing-in-itself (i.e., how something *really is*, as opposed to how it appears to a human observer), and Hegel essentially re-closes that gap by claiming to find a 'higher synthesis' between these opposed poles. Žižek argues that this is a misreading. The so-called 'synthesis' of Hegel is nothing but a new concept that refers to the gap itself – that is, to say, the synthesis between the poles represents a shift toward accepting the very gap between them.

One can express the relationship between Kant and Hegel in dialectical terms that are very similar to the dialectical approach to the problem of basing society on reality laid out in the previous chapter. At the risk of oversimplifying, one can say that modern philosophers before Kant believed that reality was inherently rational and could, at least in principle, be fully known by the human mind. (This is parallel to the position that it is possible to base society on reality.) Under the influence of Hume, Kant accepted that it is impossible for human reason to fully grasp reality and set about analysing the structure of human reason to demonstrate the precise sense in which this was true. Yet, just like the position that human society can only approximate, but never ultimately reach, full correspondence with reality, Kant is still viewing his new discovery from within the old frame. Hegel doesn't re-close the gap so much as radicalize it, by removing the frame and effectively replacing the concept of 'reality' with the concept of the Real – what appears to be a gap in our human knowledge is actually the inherent lack that is the Real itself. Or to say the same thing in Žižek's Lacanian terms: we cannot fully grasp the Real because the Real is non-all. In principle, then,

Kant 'discovered sexual difference' insofar as his antinomies anticipate the logic of the (masculine) constitutive exception and the (feminine) non-all – but it took Hegel to carry Kant's revolutionary discovery to its logical conclusion by shifting from an epistemological obstacle into an ontological fault, from the lack in our knowledge to the lack in being itself.[11]

The 'vanishing mediator'

Kant's antinomies arose out of his attempt to grasp the paradoxes of human self-consciousness or subjectivity. The structure of 'sexual difference' – the 'masculine' constitutive exception and 'feminine' non-all – is in turn reflected in the subject itself. Above, I noted that the feminine non-all of the Real is more primordial than the masculine logic of the constitutive exception that seeks to cope with it. On the level of the subject, the feminine is also more primordial, serving as a 'vanishing mediator' – a term that Žižek always leaves in scare-quotes – in the establishment of the symbolic structure, at which point the masculine subject becomes a subordinate part of the overall order. Philosophically, Žižek sees this logic at work in Descartes, the founding figure of modern philosophy.[12] In his *Meditations on First Philosophy*, Descartes is seeking a way to establish all of his knowledge on a firm basis and determines to follow the path of methodological doubt. The classic definition of the modern subject arises when Descartes finds the first building block of certain knowledge in his famous statement 'I think, therefore I am', *cogito ergo sum*. After that, he is able to determine that God exists and therefore that his senses are not systematically deceiving him – in short, he is able to establish a philosophical system where the subject as *res cogitans*, 'thinking thing', has its own particular place. But in order to get to his first building block, Descartes must first descend into the void of absolute doubt, in which he does not know whether he is in a dream, whether he is being systematically deceived by an evil demon, or even whether he exists or not. This moment of sheer madness in which Descartes determines to doubt absolutely everything is the empty self-relating *cogito*, and the *ergo sum* is Descartes' subsequent attempt to find some way out of the terrifying abyss of pure subjectivity.[13]

For Žižek, the empty void is subjectivity at its most radical, and despite its wholly negative character, it is an absolutely necessary step in the foundation of any order. This dual concept of the subject opens up a shift of perspective. In the previous chapter, my explanation of the relationship among the subject, the big Other and the Real in Žižek's early phase was centred on the big Other as basically 'always already there' – the big Other confronts the subject as something already existing and offers the forced choice of either giving up *jouissance* or becoming psychotic. This approach reflected the origins of Žižek's approach in a critique of Althusser, for whom the subject is an after-effect of ideology. The shift toward German Idealism in this phase of his work is also a shift toward the subject as 'the spontaneous transcendent agent that constitutes reality',[14] reality (for our purposes in this chapter) being understood primarily as the big Other. That is to say, the concept of the feminine subject as 'vanishing mediator' provides the key for answering the question, quoted at the beginning of this chapter, of how the big Other arises in the first place.

Žižek's most extended and systematic account of the creation of the big Other comes in *The Indivisible Remainder*. The book begins with a reading of the drafts of Schelling's unfinished *Weltalter* ['Ages of the World'] project, a work of speculative theology which Žižek nonetheless calls 'the founding text of dialectical materialism'.[15] These texts attempt to account for the rational ordering of the universe, which for Schelling cannot be taken as a simple given. Instead, 'the primordial, radically contingent fact, a fact which can in no way be accounted for, is freedom itself, a freedom bound by nothing, a freedom which, in a sense, *is* Nothing; and the problem is, rather, how this Nothing of the abyss of primordial freedom becomes entangled in the causal chains of Reason'.[16] I will discuss what Žižek takes to be the full consequences of the primordiality of freedom, along with his attempts to bring this perspective into line with contemporary science, in my fourth chapter, on dialectical materialism. For the purposes of the current chapter, the important thing to note is that in Schelling's account, there is no way to jump straight from the abyss of freedom into a rational order – some middle step, some 'vanishing mediator', is necessary.

In the *Weltalter*, Schelling is in a sense attempting to answer the

Subjectivity and ethics

age-old question of what God was doing before the creation of the world. In contrast to the famous answer often attributed to Martin Luther – 'creating hell for the curious' – Schelling argues that God was *becoming God*. In Žižek's reading, the steps are as follows. First, before the beginning, there is an abyss of pure Freedom, pure undifferentiated potentiality. In a sense, this abyss *is* God, but it is more precise to say that it is not yet God. At this stage, (pre-)God is a pure will, willing nothing in particular. This stasis is interrupted when God switches from willing *nothing* in particular to willing *nothingness itself*, producing a radical contraction that then explodes into a will for expansion, that is, an attempt at willing something in particular.[17] Before becoming the Creator, then, God *contracts* Being, in the dual sense (mirrored in Schelling's German) of a contraction as an abbreviation or condensation and of contracting a disease. In this moment, God is already a subject, in the sense of a self-relating negativity, but is stuck in a continual vicious circle of expansion and contraction. This vicious circle is what Žižek calls 'drive', which is not so much irrational as pre-rational, a series of failed attempts to establish rationality: 'Prior to the Beginning, there is in a sense only the failed Beginning [. . .].'[18] God is only able to escape from the vicious circle of drive by pronouncing his Word. The Word represents a moment of decision, which expels drive into the eternal past and gives God his basic consistency as God and opens up the horizon of time by drawing a permanent dividing line between past and present.[19] In a sense, then, instead of eternity being the higher goal of time, time is an escape from eternity: 'The Absolute "opens up time", it "represses" the rotary motion into the past, in order to get rid of the antagonism in its heart which threatens to drag it into the abyss of madness . . . *eternity itself begets time in order to resolve the deadlock it became entangled in*.'[20] Yet once made, this choice can never become conscious, because that would undo the fragile balance by which God had established himself. To reverse Luther's quip, then, one might say that for Schelling, before creating the world, God was *escaping from* hell.

This mythical account – which is plainly 'wrong' from both a materialist standpoint, at least as that is normally understood, and from an orthodox Christian standpoint – is important for Žižek because of the explicit parallels that it draws between God and the human subject. For Schelling, humanity is the point in creation where the primordial freedom breaks out once again, and each human subject repeats God's act of choosing himself. Schelling argues that even though each person must be considered responsible for her own character (i.e., must be considered to have chosen to be the person she is), the choice of character is radically unconscious, which Schelling conceptualizes in terms of a past that always remains irreducibly past and can never be called up into present conscious awareness. In a paragraph that Žižek frequently quotes in subsequent works, Schelling says,

> The deed, once accomplished, sinks immediately into the unfathomable depth, thereby acquiring its lasting character. It is the same with the will which, once posited at the beginning and led into the outside, immediately has to sink into the unconscious. This is the only way the beginning, the beginning that does not cease to be one, the truly eternal beginning, is possible. For here also it holds that the beginning should not know itself. Once done, the deed is eternally done. The decision that is in any way the true beginning should not appear before consciousness, it should not be recalled to mind, since this, precisely, would amount to its recall. He who, apropos of a decision, reserves for himself the right to drag it again to light, will never accomplish anything.[21]

Paradoxically, then, human beings all predestine *themselves*. For Žižek, the psychoanalytic parallel for this auto-predestination is the construction of the fundamental fantasy.[22] The most primordial mode of human subjectivity is a sheer void of self-relating negativity, parallel to Descartes' 'insane' radical doubt. This empty subject is caught in the vicious cycle of drive, unable to gain a stable distance from its own *jouissance*. The subject 'pronounces a Word' by choosing its fundamental fantasy, giving it a workable distance from its *jouissance* and expelling the fantasy into the unconscious (or the 'eternal' past that can never become present).

As discussed in the previous chapter, the 'fallout' of the imposition of the fundamental fantasy is *objet petit a* as the remainder of *jouissance* that is simultaneously the subject's innermost core and what the subject can never reach. In *Indivisible Remainder*, Žižek claims that *objet a* is ultimately the subject's own eternal decision. Contrary to the traditional psychoanalytic view of the unconscious as the irrational 'id', Žižek argues that 'what is truly "unconscious" in man is not the immediate opposite of consciousness, the obscure and confused "irrational" vortex of drives, but the very founding gesture of consciousness, the act of decision by which I "choose myself" – that is, combine this multitude of drives into the unity of my Self'.[23] Even though this gesture of decision is absolutely necessary for some kind of self-consistency to emerge, the encounter with this decision is unbearably traumatic once order has been established. This is not only because, in this theory of subjectivity, madness is more primordial than reason. More radically, the decision is traumatic because the imposition of order on madness *is itself insane*. The act by which the standards of reason are decided cannot, by definition, be judged by the standards it imposes.[24] Here again we see the logic of the feminine 'vanishing mediator', the necessary intermediate agency that disappears or is 'repressed' in the very moment of its success.

Fantasy and the big Other

The present discussion may seem to be very distant from the stated goal of attempting to account for the rise of the big Other. All the talk of the subject's self-establishment – and particularly the analogy between the subject and God – may seem to some to indicate the worst kind of individualism, a failing often associated with both psychoanalysis and German Idealism. This extended analysis of the structure of subjectivity, however, provides a way to get at the overlap – which in the last chapter was pointed out but not explained – between the fundamental fantasy and the big Other. For Žižek, 'sexual difference', the division of the subject between the feminine 'vanishing mediator' of decision (the pure *cogito*) and the stable masculine subject (the *ergo sum*), means that the subject is never fully self-transparent. This opacity of the subject, the fact that it can never find its elusive meaning in itself, drives it to seek that meaning in another subject – which is, in turn, also opaque to it (and to itself). Here the situation is parallel to the hypothetical endless signifying chain from the first chapter: unable to find its meaning in itself, the subject attempts to find that meaning in the other, but the other is only able to find its meaning in *another* other . . . and so on to eternity, never landing on any shared basis for interaction.

The big Other arises out of this situation through a reversal: 'instead of endlessly pursuing the hopeless search for some positive common denominator, I *presuppose this denominator as already present*'.[25] Obviously this is a deception, but it is a deception that is necessary for the symbolic order as the shared social realm to arise: 'for Meaning to emerge, it must be presupposed as already given'. For this reason, the identification with the master signifier at bottom has nothing to do with its concrete content, but is rather '*identification with the very gesture of identification*'.[26] This movement of anticipatory identification is not something that is added over against the structure of subjectivity, but stems directly from that structure. If human subjects were transparent to themselves and to each other, then the virtual order of the big Other would not be necessary: we would automatically know how to interact with each other. It is because subjects are opaque to themselves and to each other that they must posit the big Other. Paradoxically, they must posit it precisely *as* always-already existing over against every individual subject, that is, they must install it as something that was always presupposed – effectively covering over the 'vanishing mediator' of its installation.

The next turn of the screw is that the big Other that we must posit to supplement our non-transparency is *itself* non-transparent. In the first chapter, I explained that fantasy was the big Other's way of binding the subject to itself. The move toward the subject allows Žižek, primarily in *The Plague of Fantasies*, to elaborate the ways in which the big Other reflects the subject's division into the surface-level ('masculine') self and the unconscious fantasy. This structure was already visible in the contradiction that 'everyone knows' that money is just paper and yet everyone still acts in accordance with the fantasy that money directly embodies value itself. The most fundamental division, however – both for Žižek's ethical thought generally and for understanding his use of theology – is between the 'official' moral law and its inherent transgression. It is easy to misunderstand the significance of this 'inherent transgression'. After all, doesn't the definition of a law necessarily imply what it would mean to transgress it? This is visible in Christian orthodoxy: along with the official 'correct' position, there is also a series of officially recognized heresies or ways of deviating from orthodoxy (Gnosticism, Docetism, Arianism, Manichaeism, etc.). After orthodoxy was well established, the first impulse upon learning of a new deviation was to attempt to understand it in terms of one of the classical heresies. This is most visible in the response to the rise of Islam, but there are also more recent cases: for instance, Dietrich Bonhoeffer diagnosed nineteenth-century Liberal Protestantism as a form of Docetism,[27] and some have claimed that George W. Bush adheres to a form of 'Manichaean dualism'.

For Žižek, however, the 'inherent transgression' goes beyond simply defining transgression to actively *inciting* transgression. That is to say, the appropriate theological reference here is not the development of orthodoxy, but Paul's argument in Romans 7 – which, as the next chapter will discuss, Žižek himself later comes to read in these very terms. At its most fundamental, the concept of the 'inherent transgression' entails a reversal of the notion of the superego. In popular Freudianism, the superego is basically equivalent to a guilty conscience, an internalized demanding authority that constantly torments the subject. In Lacan, however, the superego becomes more insidious – rather than a constant demand to obey the exacting moral law, the superego's ultimate command is: 'Like it or not, enjoy yourself!'[28] This injunction to enjoy operates at the level of fantasy and therefore can never explicitly come to the surface: 'In order to be operative, fantasy has to remain "implicit", it has to maintain a distance toward the explicit symbolic texture sustained by it, and to function as its inherent transgression.'[29] Thus, particularly in his later works on Christianity, Žižek refers to this command to enjoy as the 'obscene superego supplement' – 'obscene' because it flagrantly contradicts the 'official' moral law, but a 'supplement' because it serves as an unspoken subtext that binds subjects to the moral law.

Though on the surface the idea of the 'obscene superego supplement' appears to be a contradiction of the conventional notion of the superego, the commandment to enjoy clarifies exactly how the guilty conscience operates. This is most clear in the explanation it offers of the frequently observed fact that the most scrupulous and moral people are also most tormented by conscience. These people essentially get caught in a feedback loop between the 'official' moral law and the obscene superego supplement. The 'official' morality disallows enjoyment, for example sexual indulgence, and so the scrupulous subject does everything possible in order to avoid this forbidden *jouissance*. In certain cases, the moral subject's attempt to avoid all sexual temptation may lead them to live in the wilderness, away from all human contact. Yet this does nothing to stop the flow of sexual thoughts, which themselves represent a violation of the moral law. Finally, the ascetic ends up performing heroic acts of self-flagellation – for instance, St Jerome is supposed to have pounded his chest with a rock every time he had an unclean thought – but, paradoxically, the ascetic exercises *themselves* take on a quasi-erotic charge. The 'guilty conscience' in this case leads to results that most people would agree are obviously 'unhealthy', yet at bottom, the subject *really is* guilty of partaking of the forbidden *jouissance*. The attempt to escape the superego injunction to enjoy only shows forth more clearly the fact that ideology (in this case, moral law) is grounded in *jouissance*.

For most people, things don't get so out of hand. This is because the moral law offers various 'release valves', violations of the law that are unofficially encouraged so that subjects can indulge in a bit of *jouissance*. Some of these 'release valves' are loopholes or other technicalities in the law whereby one can violate the spirit of the law while adhering to the letter – and often these loopholes will provide lawmakers with an opportunity to give favours to a particular constituency while still 'keeping up appearances'. More significantly, there are often situations where it is generally understood that authority will look the other way if a particular law is violated. A good example of this is the near-universal violation of speed limit laws in the United States. In many jurisdictions, the effective speed limit, i.e., the one the police will actually enforce, is ten to fifteen miles per hour higher than the posted limit. Common sense would seem to dictate that the speed limits should be set to more realistic levels, but maintaining the official limits allows everyone to 'keep up appearances' of being concerned for fuel conservation and highway safety,

Subjectivity and ethics

while the selective literal application of the speed limit laws also provides police with the pretext to stop members of racial minorities and search their vehicles ('racial profiling'). Another example is tolerating prostitution as a way to give married men a 'release valve' other than a long-term affair, which would pose more of a danger of breaking up a marriage – or more horrifically, the lynching of African-Americans in the southern United States in the wake of emancipation, where authorities tolerated (or even directly participated in) mob violence and extra-legal 'executions' as the necessary price of keeping blacks 'in their place'. That is to say, murder, the most serious possible crime, was countenanced as a way of maintaining the underlying racist fantasy.

In all these cases, the ideological fantasy serves as a kind of implied commentary on the moral law, telling the subject which rules to take seriously and, in general, how to apply the law. The result is that ideology ends up offering the subject a series of 'forced choices'. The most fundamental forced choice, of course, is that discussed in the previous chapter: either submit to the ideological order or fail to 'exist' as a social subject. Even in everyday life, however, there are many things that are 'technically' allowed, but that amount to empty gestures that are not intended to be taken seriously.[30] Žižek frequently uses the example of asking people 'how they are doing' – it is merely done out of politeness, and if someone takes the question seriously and begins going into detail about how they really are doing, it is experienced as an intrusion.[31] Another example is the boss who wants to appear to be open to criticism and tells his employees that they can come to him any time to openly discuss anything that's on their mind. 'Everyone knows' that he doesn't really want to hear criticisms, but this token gesture alone can be enough to guarantee the boss a reputation for being very open to employee concerns. This last example also demonstrates the fact that ideology often includes 'authentic' values, which is to say, no ideology is ever 'purely' ideological – and in fact, this 'trans-ideological kernel' is absolutely essential to the functioning of ideology, as long as it is not taken too seriously.[32]

Thus, to review, surreptitiously violating the law does not subvert the existing order, but is directly *incited* – when the subject starts to find the law overly demanding, 'the solemn agent of

Power suddenly starts to wink at us across the table in a gesture of obscene solidarity, letting us know that the thing (i.e. his orders) is not to be taken too seriously, *and thereby consolidating his power*.[33] Similarly, cynical distance toward the 'official' values – for example, 'solidarity' in socialist countries or 'self-management' in Yugoslavia in particular – simply repeats the gesture of ideology, which needs recourse to these values in order to legitimate itself but at the same time can't maintain its hold on power if they are taken seriously. All of this points toward Žižek's preferred strategy for undermining ideology: simply take it literally.[34] Žižek's favoured example is of course the fall of Real Socialism, but perhaps a more familiar example can be found in the African-American Civil Rights Movement. Martin Luther King, Jr's strategy of nonviolent resistance was, on the literal level, in violation of the law, but it was based in an appeal to the most fundamental principles of American ideology. Clearly, the very fact that the Civil Rights Movement was necessary illustrates that the United States did not actualize its stated ideals of human equality and freedom. Had blacks simply risen up in violent rebellion, that would have only reinforced the ideological fantasy that painted (and continues to paint) blacks as an inherently violent race that can only be subdued by coercive force. By taking American ideals literally, however, King and his followers were directly able to incite southerners to expose the terrible violence at the core of their racist ideology. Thus even though it was, at the level of the facts, based in naïve 'illusions', the Civil Rights Movement exposed the fundamental antagonisms of society. This example demonstrates in action the fact that *'ideology has nothing to do with "illusion"'*[35] – in certain cases, objectively false beliefs (i.e., that America is really all about freedom and equality) can undermine an ideological fantasy that more factual or realistic beliefs would leave untouched.

Diagnosing ethics

The complex interrelationships among the subject, the subject's *jouissance* and the big Other form the terrain on which Žižek works out his ethical thought. The ultimate identity, explained above, between *objet petit a* and the subject's own 'eternal choice of character' (i.e., of his or her own fundamental fantasy) grounds the fundamental principle of Žižekian ethics: you are responsible for your *jouissance*. In the previous chapter, I noted that *jouissance* binds the subject to ideology. The same basic insight is at play here, but the emphasis is on the subject's own complicity in and responsibility for the ideological order. This responsibility holds even in the most oppressive circumstances. For example, Žižek argues that under Communism, the party exacted a '"surplus-obedience", a gesture of compliance that was accomplished out of a pure *jouissance* provided by [one's] participation in the oppressive Communist ideological ritual'.[36] This excessive gesture of identification is nearly impossible to avoid: 'even if the actual gesture of compliance was very modest, we are dealing with "surplus-obedience" the moment the gesture of compliance provides the subject with a *jouissance* of its own'.[37]

This surplus-obedience is ultimately what founds the excessive hatred for the old regime that Žižek detects in many of the figures who were the most effective agents of the Communists: recognition of one's own surplus-obedience is humiliating.[38] Žižek goes on to apply this logic to the question of Germans' responsibility for the Holocaust, but it also finds its place in more 'normal' circumstances. For instance, many people (myself included) who have had to work in undesirable jobs just for the sake of getting by have experienced occasional moments of getting caught up in the work, doing an 'excessively' good job, and enjoying it. Once that moment is over, however, the whole affair becomes even more humiliating than before – one is no longer simply the victim of economic necessity, but has gained 'a little extra' from the situation.[39] Nevertheless, this logic should not be taken to exculpate the authorities for their role: oppression is even *more* violent when it humiliates the subject by arousing his or her *jouissance*.[40]

As these examples demonstrate, the field in which responsibility for one's own *jouissance* is played out is the big Other. In psychoanalysis, the various modes of relating to one's *jouissance* and the big Other can be divided into the four basic diagnoses – psychosis, perversion, and the two forms of neurosis: obsession and hysteria. For Žižek, Lacan raises these diagnostic categories to the level of 'existential-ontological positions' parallel to the various forms of subjectivity that Hegel analyses in *Phenomenology of Spirit* and other works.⁴¹ Following up on his insight that every theory of subjectivity implies an ethics,⁴² Žižek deploys these categories primarily as ethical stances, which are ranked according to the degree to which the subject is actually taking responsibility for his or her own *jouissance* or, as will become clearer in the next section, by the degree to which they approximate to Lacan's late notion of the psychoanalytic cure. For this reason, he does not have equal interest in every diagnosis. Most notably, he rarely discusses psychosis as such, because the psychotic subject has 'opted out' by refusing the forced choice to become subject to the symbolic order. As a result, from the perspective of Žižek's project, there is simply not much to say about psychosis, although it does implicitly come up in an interesting way in his discussions of the cure.

All along, the category of hysteria is most important, but in this stage of Žižek's thought, he begins to develop the notion of perversion in great detail. Given Žižek's generally 'edgy' approach (sexual jokes, lengthy discussions of pornography, etc.), one might expect perversion to be valorized in his work, particularly given his recent film entitled *The Pervert's Guide to Cinema* and his references to the 'perverse core of Christianity'.⁴³ In order to understand Žižek's ethical thought and in particular his work on Christianity, however, one must be absolutely clear: for Žižek, perversion names *the ultimate ethical failure*. Žižek defines the pervert as one who makes himself the instrument of the Other's *jouissance*. This means that he identifies directly with the obscene superego supplement, 'reading between the lines' of the official ideological text and realizing that the moral law actually *needs* transgression: 'The pervert is thus the "inherent transgressor" *par excellence*: he brings to light, stages, practices the secret fantasies that sustain the predominant public discourse.'⁴⁴ Since the ideological fantasy is what sustains the 'official' moral law, the pervert reinforces the law, and indeed even requires it, since perverse enjoyment depends on violating the stated law.⁴⁵ Hence the motto: 'Perversion is not subversion'.⁴⁶

Although this term originally referred to homosexuality in psychoanalytic theory, Žižek detaches it from that context, and indeed from the sexual context altogether,⁴⁷ applying the term primarily to political situations. The most obvious example is religious fundamentalism. The 'perversion' here isn't simply following religious teachings devoutly and using them as a guide for political practice. Instead, the problem is the way that God undergoes a split – on the one hand, there is the acceptable public face (Jesus as a 'nice guy' who taught about love), but this is underwritten by an obscene *jouissance* (the vengeful God). This results in some fairly obvious contradictions: killing doctors in the name of 'the sanctity of life', for example. In a perverse approach to religion, however, this contradiction doesn't register as such: instead, being God's instrument means that one is permitted and even encouraged to break the common moral laws in the service of a higher goal.

Žižek's own constant example of the politics of perversion is Stalinism. Although officially atheist, Stalinist ideology relies on a concept of 'historical necessity' that functions in much the same way as the fundamentalist God. On the one hand, the goal of the class struggle is to produce Communism as a transparent, self-regulating society based on reason. On the other hand, establishing this order requires extraordinary violence. Just as with the example of Christian fundamentalism, certain contradictions arise – most notably, establishing the society of solidarity requires falsely accusing one's comrades, torturing a false confession out of them, and putting them to death. Yet the reference to historical necessity allows the subject a free hand to violate all laws of morality.[48] In both cases, the perverse subject is disavowing the *jouissance* he derives from all the brutal acts he commits. This stance is arguably at its most morally bankrupt in the self-pitying torturers who are wracked with guilt because necessity has forced them to perform such immoral deeds. Their very shame betrays them – it is 'the unmistakable sign of the excess of *enjoyment* they got from their acts'.[49] Žižek's interest in Stalinism is motivated by a desire to discern precisely where it went wrong, not by a desire to return to it.

Both forms of neurosis share one basic trait that separates them from perversion: the neurotic subject does not know what the Other wants, that is, what the subject is in the eyes of the Other. This is the 'normal' attitude toward ideology, which is understandable given the self-contradictory nature of the ideological order. The difference between hysteria and obsession lies in the subject's attitude toward this uncertainty. Traditionally, obsession is said to be more common among men and hysteria to be more common among women. Here again, just as with the 'formulae of sexuation', Žižek consistently sticks to the gendered language, frequently referring to these two categories simply as 'men' and (much more frequently) 'women', even though he recognizes that either category can be found in people of either biological gender. Following the pattern of his use of gendered language thus far, Žižek shows very little interest in obsessionals or 'men'. These subjects use their uncertainty about the Other's desire or about their status in the eyes of the Other as a kind of cushion to avoid any potentially traumatic encounters or realizations.[50] An everyday manifestation of this stance is the man who suspects he has some kind of health problem, but is afraid to go to the doctor. The obsessional subject acts as though his health problem doesn't properly exist as long as he avoids an authoritative pronouncement on its status. Most often, the real fear is not that the doctor will tell him that he has a terminal disease, but that he will be required to change some aspect of his lifestyle – to give up his comfortable routine of *jouissance*. If perversion isn't subversion, then neither is obsession.

The only truly subversive subject position is that of the hysteric or 'woman'. For Žižek, the structure of hysteria is the fundamental structure of modern subjectivity as a whole, and obsession is merely a derivation, parallel to his claim that the 'feminine' subject as 'vanishing mediator' is the primordial form of subjectivity. In contrast with the obsessional, the hysterical subject desires a straight answer to the question of what she is for the Other or what the Other wants. Given the radical inconsistency and dividedness of the big Other, no such answer is available, but the search for it can produce significant disruptive effects, uncovering contradictions and instabilities that otherwise would go unnoticed. For all Žižek's high praise of the hysterical stance, however, it remains ambiguous. Most significantly, hysterical questioning tends to be formulated in terms of specific demands that take on a larger significance – somehow everything hinges on *this one thing*. As a result, the hysterical demand always has a hidden undertone: 'Don't give me what I ask of you, because that's not *it*.'[51] In some cases, this demand can offer a kind of 'master signifier' of oppression, leading to revolutionary change.

Subjectivity and ethics

Yet the strategy of hysterical provocation is fragile. On the one hand, the figure of authority can spoil the strategy by simply granting the stated demands, prematurely closing off a process whose real implications went far beyond the presenting issue. On the other hand, there can be the opposite problem of 'bombarding the [authorities] with *impossible* demands, with demands which are "made to be rejected"', meaning that ultimately nothing changes.[52] In the end, the problem with hysteria is the problem with subversion in general: it leaves the big Other in place and is in fact parasitical on the existing order. To take full responsibility for one's relationship to the big Other is to take responsibility for overthrowing and *replacing* it.

The cure

Hysteria provides a necessary starting point, but for truly revolutionary change to occur, hysteria must become more than hysteria. Here Žižek's model is Lacan's late teaching on the psychoanalytic cure. In the clinical setting, what leads a person to enter into analysis is some disturbing *symptom*: a nervous tic, for instance, or a broader pattern of self-undermining behaviour. This symptom indicates that the subject's strategy for keeping *jouissance* under control is beginning to unravel. According to Žižek's periodization, in early stages of Lacan's work, his notion of the end goal of analysis was more or less therapeutic, helping the patient to cope with the symptom in some way.[53] In the final period, however, Žižek argues that Lacan's notion of the goal of analysis was much more radical – not to 'heal' the subject's unravelling, but to carry that unravelling through to the end. More precisely, analysis serves to help the subject to arrive at the point where he or she can *choose* this unravelling.

In formal terms, the end of analysis corresponds to two related shifts: from desire to drive and from symptom to *sinthome*. In both cases, the 'content' remains the same, but a perspective shift intervenes that changes everything. As discussed in the previous chapter, desire names the subject's perpetually frustrated quest for *objet petit a*, the leftover bit of *jouissance* that constitutes the 'fallout' of the imposition of the big Other. The shift from desire to drive happens when one drops the reference to *objet a* as an elusive something 'out there'. Deprived of its supposed 'goal', desire looks like an endless repetitive circle, which is to say, desire becomes *drive*, which for Žižek is the most originary form of *jouissance*. Whereas the subject of desire is propelled by a perceived lack of *objet petit a*, for the subject of drive, the quest itself *immediately is objet petit a*. The shift from symptom to *sinthome* is a necessary correlative with the shift from desire to drive. Initially, the symptom seems to be an intrusion that disturbs one's carefully constructed self-identity. For the subject of drive, however, the symptom manifests the *jouissance* that holds the subject together. Lacan denotes this changed status of the symptom by the neologism *sinthome*, whose many connotations include *synth*esis.

These parallel shifts represent an undoing or 'going through' of the fundamental fantasy. Where the fundamental fantasy installs desire as a way of keeping *objet petit a* at bay, the collapse of desire into drive and the collapse of the symptom into the *sinthome* both amount to immediate identification between the subject and *objet a* – an identification that is called 'subjective destitution'. In essence, then, the cure consists in reversing the process that gave rise to the subject:

> The subject emerges via the 'externalization' of the most intimate kernel of its being (the 'fundamental fantasy'); the moment he gets too close to this traumatic content and 'internalizes' it, his very self-identity dissolves. For this reason, ['going through' the] fantasy and 'subjective destitution' are strictly correlative, two aspects of the same operation.[54]

The subject cannot 'consciously' choose to undergo this traumatic encounter with the fundamental fantasy. Instead, over the course of analysis, the hysteric is brought to that point indirectly, by gradually being deprived of any excuses or external supports. As noted above, hysterical provocation is parasitic on the big Other and the various holders of symbolic authority (spouse, parents, teachers, etc.). The hysteric blames the Other for her problems, which become condensed in a symptom. Analysis brings the hysteric to the point where she (at least implicitly) recognizes the fictional

Subjectivity and ethics

nature of the big Other, the fact that 'the Other doesn't exist' – not in the sense that other people aren't real, but that the Other (both the big Other and particular Others) is intrinsically inconsistent and lacking. For example, a patient who was constantly frustrated in her attempts to please her parents might come to understand that her parents themselves didn't know what they wanted from her and that the subject ultimately installed her parents' impossible demands. That is to say, the basic lack that has structured the subject's entire life is not an externally imposed wound: it is, at bottom, self-inflicted. Taking responsibility for one's fundamental fantasy – for one's *jouissance* – precipitates a collapse of the subject into its innermost kernel.

From *Sublime Object* forward, Žižek's understanding of the structure of the cure has remained basically the same. Though he does develop aspects of it in this stage – most notably the concept of drive – the truly important shift is perspectival. In the early work, as noted in the beginning of this chapter, the cure seemed tantamount to sheer self-destruction. Although Žižek's loyalty to (the later) Lacan meant that he was duty-bound to expound his notion of the cure, there is little indication of why anyone would want to undergo analysis in the first place when the supposed 'cure' sounds so much like a psychotic break. In light of his reading of Schelling in *The Indivisible Remainder*, however, the cure appears as a way of tapping back into the radical and vertiginous freedom at the origin of subjectivity. If the choice of the fundamental fantasy is an auto-predestination, then the psychoanalytic cure represents a chance to revise it, a paradoxical opportunity to re-predestine oneself. The choice of the cure thus represents a kind of 'reboot' of the subject, the installation of a new fantasy and a new stance toward the big Other – it represents 'an authentic act [which] momentarily suspends the big Other, but it is simultaneously the *"vanishing mediator" which grounds, brings into existence, the big Other*'.[55] Like the original fundamental fantasy itself, this impossible choice can never become conscious, but nonetheless paradoxically represents freedom in its most radical form.[56]

As with Lacan's diagnostic categories, Žižek's interest in the psychoanalytic cure lies ultimately in its political implications. In terms of his loyalty to the 'vanishing mediators' who brought about the fall of Communism in Eastern Europe, this Schellingian reading of the cure gives him a strong theoretical reason for his conviction that he was participating in something authentic: namely, that the political 'vanishing mediator' reenacts the abyssal freedom at the root of every social order. The anti-Communist movements also reflect the basic structure that he extracts from the notion of the cure in order to define an authentic 'act'. From the perspective of an established structure of subjectivity, the impossible encounter with the fundamental fantasy is the very worst thing that could happen. The symptom may be bad, but the complete collapse of the subject is even worse. Nevertheless, this choice of the worst is an irruption of primordial freedom that results in a complete reconfiguration of the subject. Similarly, in a political situation, the authentic act happens when 'the choice of (what, within the situation, appears as) the Worst changes the very standards of what is good or bad'.[57] In terms of the Communist situation, the obvious options for those who found the regime intolerable would be to expose the system's lies or to take up arms, whereas the decision to take the ideology literally seems to be a naïve and even crazy choice of playing directly into the regime's hands. Nevertheless, this choice of the worst option ended up completely reconfiguring the situation. This combination of the destructive with the liberatory is what leads Žižek, following Lacan, to designate the authentic act as the moment of 'death drive'.

For the most part, Žižek's examples of the authentic act in this stage are individual rather than political. His most frequently used example is the character Sygne de Coufontaine, from Paul Claudel's play *The Hostage*,[58] an example that Lacan himself analysed at great length. That example ends with the character's death, and Žižek gives no indication that any political consequences followed – the point is rather to show that the authentic act is ultimately gratuitous, that no 'reason' can be given for it. Most of his other examples are less extreme, though sharing the general structure of opening up a seemingly hopeless situation by unexpectedly choosing an 'insane' course of action. In the interests of providing a broadly familiar example, it might be helpful to refer to my favourite parable of Jesus, the parable of the dishonest manager.[59] Jesus presents a manager who has been caught stealing from his master and is therefore told he is going to be fired. The manager has very few options once he loses his job, and so one might expect him to try to convince his master he didn't really cheat him or to beg for mercy – but instead the manager decides to *cheat his master even more*. Using the little time he has left, he calls in his master's debtors and reduces their debt, in the hopes that they will be favourably disposed toward him and 'welcome him into their homes'[60] – perhaps meaning offer him a new job. This 'insane' self-destructive move of digging himself even deeper is so unexpected that even the defrauded master himself can't help but admire the manager's brilliant strategy.

Though Žižek does not use this example himself, it does point toward a serious question about his work up to this point: in the end, is the cured subject simply trading masters? Aside from claiming that the moment of vertiginous freedom is inherently 'worth it', is there any way of assessing if anything has been gained in this process? As the next chapter will show, Žižek only confronts these questions head-on in his encounter with Alain Badiou, and his engagement with theology represents his initial attempt to answer them.

Chapter 3
The Christian experience

This chapter deals directly with Žižek's engagement with theology. Both of the previous chapters have served as a necessary preparation for this one, introducing the most important Lacanian concepts and explaining the impasses that led Žižek to deepen and reorder his understanding of those concepts and the interrelationships among them. In a book entitled *Žižek and Theology*, however, I could have taken a different route. Every one of his books includes theological references, and so I could have simply made note of these, perhaps organizing my reflections around key theological themes or figures. My reason for not doing this is that, as I observed in the introduction, Žižek's references to Christianity in earlier periods tended to be 'mere examples', relatively straightforward illustrations drawn from a shared cultural heritage or, more often, directly from his sources. As noted in the first chapter, Žižek's use of Pascal in *Sublime Object*, for instance, was prompted by Althusser's references in 'Ideology and Ideological State Apparatuses'. His main source for Christian references, however, is Hegel, in whose philosophy Christianity played a central role. With two important exceptions that I will note below, someone interested in understanding Žižek's early use of theology would be best served by reading a study of Hegel's approach to theology.

In the works under consideration in this chapter, however, something different is at work. Here Žižek is developing his own idiosyncratic understanding of the origin of Christianity and its relationship to paganism and Judaism. He works this out over the course of three books – *The Fragile Absolute* (2000), *On Belief* (2001) and *The Puppet and the Dwarf* (2003) – which were all published in a relatively short period and which sometimes disagree with each other on key points. The most obvious shift is in his attitude toward Buddhism. In *The Fragile Absolute*, he sometimes valorizes Buddhism in parallel with Christianity;[1] in *On Belief*, he argues that the reference to Buddhism is a red herring for Westerners because looking elsewhere for 'ancient wisdom' is actually the most characteristically Western gesture;[2] and in *The Puppet and the Dwarf*, he is actively (and to my mind, strangely disproportionately) hostile toward Buddhism.[3] Yet even on central questions such as the relationship between Judaism and Christianity and the role of Paul, Žižek's thinking undergoes noticeable changes over the course of the three books. All of this shows that religion had no preordained place in his project.

Though he does ultimately ground his own understanding of Christian origins in terms of Lacan and Hegel, it is not simply a question of 'applying' his system to Christianity, as Badiou arguably does in his book on Paul.[4] Instead, as I've been arguing, his appropriation of theology is a way of working out a shift in his project. Broadly speaking, his psychoanalytically inflected retelling of the story of Christian origins is Žižek's way of answering the question of 'the morning after': 'it is easy to suspend the big Other by means of the act *qua* real, to experience the "nonexistence of the big Other" in a momentary flash – however, what do we do *after* we have traversed the fantasy?'[5] As previous chapters have shown, Žižek's initial answer is simply to establish a new big Other, but the obvious problem that then arises is how to assess if the whole affair has been 'worth it'. For Žižek, the act or 'vanishing mediator' as a moment of radical freedom is of course intrinsically valuable. Yet is there any way to remain faithful to that moment if the imposition of a new master signifier always covers over the 'vanishing mediator'?

Žižek first tackles this question in a serious way in *The Ticklish Subject* when he discusses Alain Badiou's notion of the truth-event. In the wake of this discussion, Badiou will increasingly become an indispensable point of reference for Žižek's work. Although a detailed assessment of the relation between the two lies outside the mandate of this book, it is necessary to dispel what I take to be some common misunderstandings. First, one must note that Žižek is highly critical of Badiou's theory in *The Ticklish Subject*, a pattern that continues in his subsequent works. Nevertheless, it is clear that Badiou is more than simply an intellectual punching-bag for Žižek, and Žižek's deep respect for Badiou

The Christian experience

has led some observers to claim that he is essentially a disciple, advocating and popularizing Badiou's philosophy. In my view, however, Badiou is less a direct source for Žižek than a catalyst to further development, and his initial reading of Badiou provides a case in point. Žižek ultimately ends up vindicating Lacan against Badiou's critiques, but in the process Žižek's reading of Lacan changes. Certainly there are cases where Žižek's 'critique' of another thinker amounts to a reassertion of Žižek's own preexisting position, but in the case of Badiou, developing an effective critique requires him to enter into new territory.

What is particularly interesting about this encounter for the purposes of this book is that Žižek's critique of Badiou is mediated through Badiou's reading of Paul as the 'founder of Christianity' – leading directly to Žižek's development, in the years immediately following, of his own counter-reading of Paul's founding gesture and of the emergence of Christianity more generally. In principle, it seems, Žižek could just as easily have critiqued Badiou and developed his own counter-position in 'purely theoretical' terms. Yet Žižek argues that there is an inner necessity to this turn to theology, going so far as to claim in *The Puppet and the Dwarf* that 'to become a true dialectical materialist, one should go through the Christian experience'.[6] To understand what prepared Žižek to be so responsive to Badiou's use of theological language and ultimately so strident in his own appropriation of it, I will begin this chapter by examining two passages from his earlier work that 'foreshadow' Žižek's theological turn: his reading of Walter Benjamin in *Sublime Object* and his defence of Schelling's use of theological language in *Indivisible Remainder*. I will then discuss Žižek's critique of Badiou in *The Ticklish Subject* and the change in position it entails. The remainder of the chapter will consist of an expository presentation of Žižek's understanding of 'the Christian experience', discussing in turn his treatment of the problem of perversion, the distinctiveness of Judaism, and the emergence of Christianity. For purposes of clarity, I will be reading the other two books on Christianity in terms of *The Puppet and the Dwarf*, as it represents the position that he carries forward into *The Parallax View*. The next chapter will conclude my presentation of Žižek's intellectual trajectory, following up on 'the Christian experience' with a discussion of 'dialectical materialism'.

Žižek and Theology

Prefiguring the theological turn

Žižek's reading of Walter Benjamin's 'Theses on the Philosophy of History'[7] is found in the shortest chapter of *Sublime Object*, entitled 'You Only Die Twice'.[8] There he begins by connecting Lacan's notion of the death drive with his various approaches to the psychoanalytic cure, linking the two concepts to the theory of revolution, all of which clearly anticipates many of the themes covered in my previous chapter. Here he brings these concepts together by contrasting the psychoanalytic concept of history with the everyday view. In the commonsense standpoint, history is a continuous series of events that can, at least in principle, be accounted for in a narrative form, whereas in Žižek's psychoanalytic perspective, human history is punctuated by a series of interruptions that dissolve and rebuild the symbolic order – that is, history is defined by the death drive, which is the non-narrative kernel or 'degree zero' of history.[9]

Žižek argues that Benjamin's 'Theses' represent the only point in Marxist theory where the non-historical moment of death drive is brought to bear in historical analysis. For Benjamin, the 'common-sense' view of history corresponds to 'the gaze of "those who have won": it sees history as a closed continuity of "progression" leading to the reign of those who rule today'. The truly Marxist or proletarian view, however, focuses on 'what *failed* in history, what has to be denied so that the continuity of "what really happened" could establish itself'.[10] More specifically, for Benjamin: 'what specifies historical materialism – in contrast to the Marxist doxa [or common opinion] according to which we must grasp events in the totality of their interconnection and in their dialectical movement – is its capacity to *arrest*, to *immobilize* historical movement and to *isolate* the detail from its historical totality'.[11] The isolated detail is the moment of past failure, and the dissolution of the historical totality established by the victors allows the historical materialist to conceive of 'the contemporary revolutionary situation . . . as a repetition of past failed situations, as their retroactive "redemption"'.[12] Žižek argues that this moment of redeeming the past is what Benjamin is getting at with his reference to 'theology' in his famous first thesis. There Benjamin envisions an unbeatable chess-playing puppet that is secretly controlled by an ugly dwarf and interprets the scenario as follows: 'One can imagine a philosophical counterpart to this device. The puppet called "historical materialism" is to win all the time. It can easily be a match for anyone if it enlists the service of theology, which today, as we know, is wizened and has to keep out of sight.'[13] Žižek returns to this thesis in *The Puppet and the Dwarf*, arguing that now the situation has reversed – historical materialism must be hidden beneath a theological surface.[14]

Benjamin's concept of revolution as a moment of stoppage goes hand in hand with his conception of history as radically open, as a 'series of events which "will have been" – their meaning, their historical dimension, is decided afterwards, through their inscription in the symbolic network'.[15] This concept of history stands in stark contrast with that of Stalinism, which converts the historical standpoint of the oppressed into 'that of a *victor* whose final triumph is guaranteed in advance by the "objective necessity of history"'.[16] For the Stalinist subject every event – past, present and future – already has its fixed or 'objective' meaning for the 'big Other' of historical necessity.[17] As discussed in the previous chapter, Žižek will later analyse this conception of history as a species of 'perversion', by which the subject abdicates his or her own responsibility in the face of some Other. Benjamin's historical materialist, by contrast, embodies a radical stance of taking responsibility *even for the past*, whose meaning will be determined by the outcome of the present struggle. Žižek aligns this structure of interruption and retroactive meaning with his own understanding of the Hegelian dialectic, over against the typical 'evolutionist' approach to the dialectic that he associates with Stalin.[18]

By the end of the chapter in question, Benjamin has faded from view as Žižek turns his attention toward contrasting Stalinism with democracy, extolling the radical openness of the democratic system and (as noted in my first chapter) claiming that elections represent an 'irruption of the Real'.[19] Nevertheless, the basic insights that Žižek extracts from Benjamin's 'Theses' – the openness of the past and the idea of revolution as an interruption – will come back again and again. The contrast with Stalin also reaches a strange culmination when, in *The Parallax View*, Žižek claims that Benjamin did not commit suicide but was killed by agents under orders from Stalin. The reason is that Benjamin was carrying a manuscript that developed at length the implicit critique of Stalinism found in the 'Theses': 'Stalin read Benjamin's "Theses", he knew about the new book project based on the "Theses", and he wanted to prevent its publication at any cost.'[20] This story is based on a news story that does not appear to have shaken the mainstream view that Benjamin committed suicide to avoid being sent to the concentration camps,[21] and in light of Žižek's subsequent discussion in *Parallax View*, it is unclear to me whether he himself thinks it is literally true. Nevertheless, his attraction to the story demonstrates that he has maintained his view of Benjamin's 'Theses', complete with its theological moves, as a devastating critique of Stalin. More broadly, Žižek's reading of Paul, as also of Lenin, has a Benjaminian tone – Paul and Lenin are interesting as moments of emergence that are ultimately betrayed.

Another foreshadowing of the theological turn comes in *The Indivisible Remainder*. As noted in the previous chapter, Žižek claims Schelling's *Weltalter* drafts as 'the founding text of dialectical materialism'.[22] In light of the common view of 'materialism', one might expect Žižek to somehow explain away the obvious theological content of Schelling's texts, but instead, Žižek claims that it is necessary to what Schelling is doing: 'the need for the form of mythical narrative arises when one endeavors to break the circle of the symbolic order and to give an account of its genesis ("origins") from the Real and its pre-symbolic antagonism'.[23] This principle can be understood as a radicalization of his principle that sometimes objectively 'false' ideas are the only way to escape the terms of the fundamental fantasy. In Schelling's case, a myth that is clearly 'wrong', both from a materialist position (as normally conceived) and from the position of orthodox Christian theology, becomes the vehicle for Schelling to expose the logic of the 'vanishing mediator', a vehicle that is not simply disposable:

> The point is not to reject what is not true in Schelling, the false ('obscurantist,' 'theosophico-mythological') shell of his system, in order to attain its kernel of truth; its truth, rather, is inextricably linked to what, from our contemporary perspective, cannot but appear as blatantly 'not true,' so that every attempt to discard the part or aspect considered 'not true' inevitably entails the loss of the truth itself . . .[24]

The Christian experience

In its immediate context, this principle applies primarily to the psychoanalytic 'myths' of Lacan and especially Freud: the murder of the primordial father by the prehistoric horde in *Totem and Taboo*, for instance. Yet it accords very well with Žižek's decision to treat Badiou's use of Paul as more than a mere 'example' of the truth-event – and to develop his own understanding of the truth-event in terms of a retelling of Christian origins that is in some sense a 'myth', insofar as few biblical scholars would endorse his reading as historically accurate.

These two passages seem to me to be connected in ways beyond their both pointing forward to Žižek's theological turn – for instance, Žižek's Schellingian reading of the psychoanalytic cure as a 're-predestination' coheres with Benjamin's notion of the historical materialist as taking responsibility also for the past. More generally, both Schelling's and Benjamin's texts – not despite their theological content, but precisely insofar as they are theological – are key points of reference for Žižek's project of developing a dialectical materialism, as I will discuss in the next chapter. Their primary importance in the present context, however, is their role as a preparation for Žižek's encounter with Badiou, to which I now turn.

A politics of truth

Badiou's theory of the truth-event is not initially attractive to Žižek *because* of Badiou's use of Paul. Rather, at the risk of exaggeration, what attracts Žižek to Badiou is ultimately what attracts him to Lacan: a concern with truth. For Žižek, 'postmodern' philosophy is parallel to the sophists of ancient Greece and the sceptics who preceded Kant – all three groups refuse to deal with the notion of truth. In many circles, Lacan is regarded as part of a kind of 'holy trinity' of postmodernism (along with Derrida and Foucault), but Žižek argues that this label is partially misleading. Lacan *is* in agreement with 'postmodernism' insofar as he recognizes that there is no going back to some pre-modern 'traditional' notion of truth. Where he departs from postmodernism is with the concept of the Real, which represents, as it were, a 'post-postmodern' concept of truth.[25] On the political level, Žižek argues that the mainstream of Western politics is afflicted by a similar problem: any political project that claims to be based on truth is dismissed as potentially totalitarian.²⁶ As previous chapters have shown, Žižek of course agrees that totalitarianism, which he analyses in terms of the psychoanalytic category of 'perversion', is an extremely negative thing. He argues that liberalism, far from preventing totalitarianism, actually ends up inciting it, as demonstrated in his theory of nationalism in *Tarrying*. In *The Ticklish Subject*, his philosophical goal is to vindicate his Lacanian notion of subjectivity against other major schools of thought, but his more important goal is political: 'While this book is philosophical in its basic tenor, it is first and foremost an engaged political intervention, addressing the burning question of how we are to reformulate a leftist, anti-capitalist political project in our era of global capitalism and its ideological supplement, liberal-democratic multi-culturalism.'²⁷

In short, *The Ticklish Subject* undertakes to develop a politics out of Žižek's theory of subjectivity, one that will break out of the current political configuration. Though he also deals with Heidegger, Judith Butler and a wide range of French leftist thinkers, Žižek signals already in the introduction the overriding importance of Badiou. While Žižek 'reject[s] his criticism of Lacan – that is, his thesis that psychoanalysis is not able to provide the foundation of a new political practice', Badiou's philosophy nonetheless represents an attempt at a politics of truth parallel to Žižek's.²⁸ A trained mathematician and student of Lacan, Badiou shares Žižek's conviction that it is not possible to go back 'behind' the modern or postmodern turn that cut philosophy and politics from their traditional substantive moorings. Instead of a positive body, Badiou argues that truth is something that *happens*, that it is an *event*.

Giving a full account of Badiou's theory of the truth-event is beyond the scope of this book, but the broad outlines are as follows.²⁹ Each truth-event corresponds to a given situation – whether that be a political situation such as the country of France at some given time, a scientific situation governed by a certain research paradigm, an artistic situation governed by certain norms or expectations, or a set of personal relationships. All elements in that situation are *present*, but not all of them are 'officially' recognized or *represented*. A good example of this can be found in the political situation: basically all countries contain people who live

The Christian experience

there without being officially recognized as citizens or legal residents. No matter the type of situation, this excluded element, with no 'official' place in the situation, is the site from which a truth-event erupts – but always unpredictably.

When the truth-event happens, some people will ignore it, others will deny that it's happening, but some will embrace it. Those who embrace the truth-event are *subjects* in the proper sense of the word, and their attempt to follow out the consequences of the truth-event is called a truth-process. In terms of Badiou's reading of Paul, the resurrection of Christ is the unexpected truth-event that seizes Paul, causing him to dedicate his life to spreading the gospel. Badiou claims that Paul is merely a helpful example, but Žižek argues on the basis of Badiou's other writings that the religious example is actually an implicit paradigm for his theory of the truth-event. Žižek agrees with Badiou that the 'fable' of the resurrection cannot be taken literally, since there is no going back on the advent of science – but then the obvious objection is that the key example of a 'truth-event' is actually based on something false.[30] Rather than taking this as a reason to reject Badiou's theory, however, Žižek follows the same principle by which he defended Schelling's theological writings: he couches his critique in theological terms.

The heart of Žižek's critique of Badiou is Badiou's rejection of the Lacanian notion of death drive, which for Žižek is tantamount to 'succumbing to the *temptation of non-thought*'. As discussed in the previous chapter, 'death drive' is one of the key names for the subject as 'vanishing mediator' or self-referential negativity. In this context, it denotes the negative gesture of detaching oneself from a given situation, which Žižek argues is absolutely necessary if something new is to emerge. For Badiou, by contrast, 'The Truth-Event is simply a radically New Beginning.'[31] In theological terms, Badiou is a 'theologian of glory' who wants the resurrection without the cross – and indeed, in his book on Paul, Badiou minimizes the cross as much as possible, arguing that the cross is little else but a demonstration that Christ was really human.

The question of death drive also leads Žižek, perhaps unexpectedly, to Badiou's reading of Romans 7, a passage Lacan himself also addresses.[32] There, as noted in the previous chapter,

Paul is grappling with something akin to the notion of the inherent transgression:

> What then should we say? That the law is sin? By no means! Yet, if it had not been for the law, I would not have known sin. I would not have known what it is to covet if the law had not said, 'You shall not covet.' But sin, seizing an opportunity in the commandment, produced in me all kinds of covetousness. Apart from the law sin lies dead. I was once alive apart from the law, but when the commandment came, sin revived and I died, and the very commandment that promised life proved to be death to me. For sin, seizing an opportunity in the commandment, deceived me and through it killed me.[33]

Badiou names this logic of the inherent transgression 'death drive' and argues that Paul is looking for a way to escape from the law and thereby from the 'death drive'.[34] For Žižek, this is close to being a simple error in terminology – what Paul is discussing here is more properly called the obscene superego supplement. Rather than trying to escape the death drive, Žižek argues, 'the problem St Paul struggles with is how to avoid the trap of *perversion*, that is, of a Law that generates its transgression, since it needs it in order to assert itself as Law'.[35] Paul can be understood here as presenting the plight of a hysteric who is starting to become conscious of the contradictory character of the symbolic order. The temptation is to short-circuit this vicious cycle of law and transgression by following a principle that Paul himself was falsely accused of promoting: 'Let us do evil that good may result.'[36]

As noted in the previous chapter, this perverse approach is as far as possible from breaking out of the law – instead, it permanently closes down the space of hysterical questioning that might serve as the site of a possible break. Žižek argues that both Paul and psychoanalysis share a goal that is the exact opposite of perversion: 'a relationship that avoids the pitfalls of the superego inculpation that accounts for the "morbid" enjoyment of sin'. Yet in the wake of pointing out Badiou's misuse of the concept of the death drive in his reading of Paul, Žižek here realigns Paul with Badiou's position, arguing that for both, the way to reach 'the domain of *Love*

The Christian experience

beyond Law' – a concept that Lacan himself explicitly embraces[37] – is directly to identify with some truth-event. For Lacan, by contrast, psychoanalysis 'does not already *posit* a "new harmony," a new Truth-Event; it – as it were – merely wipes the slate clean for one'.[38] Whereas Badiou argues for direct identification with the resurrection in order to escape from the obscene superego supplement, Lacan claims that one must 'die to the law', that is, submit to 'symbolic death' through traversing the fantasy and undergoing subjective destitution:

> What 'Death' stands for at its most radical is not merely the passing of earthly life, but the 'night of the world' [a phrase from Hegel that refers to the following:], the self-withdrawal, the absolute contraction of subjectivity, the severing of its links with 'reality' – *this* is the 'wiping the slate clean' that opens up the domain of the symbolic New Beginning, of the emergence of the 'New Harmony' sustained by a newly emerged Master-Signifier.[39]

In other words, in sharp contrast with Badiou the 'theologian of glory', Lacan is a good Lutheran 'theologian of the cross'.

The obvious question here is what difference the emphasis on death makes. Žižek argues here that symbolic death necessarily leads to the installation of a new master signifier or 'truth-event', and so it might seem that the Lacanian approach ultimately ends up in the same place as Badiou. The difference becomes clear when trying to answer another important question: How do I know that a truth-event is really a truth-event? In political terms, this means determining which purported revolutions are 'true' revolutions. Both Žižek and Badiou agree that the Nazi regime, though 'revolutionary' in a superficial way, is ultimately a false revolution. Badiou has various formal standards by which he believes he can exclude Nazism as a truth-event, most notably that a truth-event must be universal in scope, whereas Jews and other marginal groups clearly were not able to participate in the Nazi movement. By contrast to the positive rules Badiou sets, Žižek's notion of what constitutes the 'truth' in a truth-event coheres with his concept of subjectivity and of the Real: 'Lacan is not a postmodernist cultural relativist: there definitely *is* a difference between an authentic Truth-Event and its semblance, and this difference lies in the fact that in a Truth-Event the void of the death drive, of radical negativity, a gap that momentarily suspends the Order of Being, continues to resonate.'[40] That is to say, the 'limit-experience' of death drive 'opens up and sustains the space for the Truth-Event, yet its excess always threatens to undermine it'. In terms of Nazism, Žižek argues that a break with the capitalist order of being never occurred because the fundamental contradiction in society was misidentified as stemming from the Jews rather than from capitalism itself. As such, the Nazi 'revolution', for all its very real destructive force, was nothing but an attempt to make sure that everything remained fundamentally the same.

This standard for the truthfulness of the truth-event is based on the psychoanalytic cure, wherein the subject confronts his or her fundamental fantasy – and for Žižek, the core of the ideological fantasy in modern society is capitalism. In mining Lacan for resources that might provide a standard for taking the next step of recognizing a social grouping or collective that is faithful to the truth-event, Žižek makes a shift that is perhaps as significant as his shift in emphasis from the big Other to the subject – the shift from the subject to the analyst. In the course of analysis, the analyst acts as a kind of replacement 'big Other', and just as in the case of the standard big Other, the subject's relationship to the analyst inevitably becomes charged with *jouissance*, meaning that the analyst becomes aligned with *objet petit a* – though Žižek does not mention it in this context, this process is classically known as transferential love. Unlike the normal big Other that serves to keep *objet a* at a distance, however, the analyst's goal is to guide the subject to an encounter with *objet petit a*, resulting in subjective destitution and 'going through' the fantasy. In order to occupy this position of *objet petit a*, the analyst must first have undergone analysis and thereby *identified* with *objet a*. Thus while most subjects simply go on with their lives after the end of analysis, some subjects undergo analysis with the specific goal of becoming analysts themselves, enabling them to become *objet petit a* for another subject in the context of analysis. In his later work, however, Lacan begins to think through the possibility of a 'collective of analysts' – that is, a form of sociality beyond the analytic situation, called the 'discourse of the analyst', wherein all subjects would represent *objet petit a* to each other. Put differently, this would be a sociality based directly in *drive* rather than desire: 'instead of being caught in the vicious cycle of permanent failure, [the discourse of the analyst] affirms this gap as positive and productive: it asserts the Real of the Event as the "generator", the generating core to be encircled repeatedly by the subject's symbolic productivity'.[41] In the discourse of the analyst, Žižek has found a model for a non-ideological political practice – a significant step forward for his theory that perhaps would not have happened without Badiou's provocation.

The reign of perversion

Though their theories of the truth-event ultimately differ fundamentally, Žižek agrees with Badiou on more than simply the gesture toward a politics of truth – he also agrees that the emergence of Christianity provides the privileged example of a truth-event. In *The Ticklish Subject*, Žižek even couches his agreement with Badiou directly in terms of the Christian example, arguing that 'what we need today is the gesture that would undermine capitalist globalization from the standpoint of universal Truth, just as Pauline Christianity did to the Roman global Empire'.[42] In a sense, all three of Žižek's books on Christianity represent successive attempts to grapple with the full implications of this single line. In all three, after calling for a Pauline-style intervention in an introduction, he turns to an analysis of what it is about the contemporary situation that makes a Pauline gesture possible and necessary.

Žižek's first attempt, in *The Fragile Absolute*, works within the same basic framework that Badiou uses in his *Saint Paul*. There Badiou depicts the contemporary world as dominated by two principles. On the one hand, there is global capitalism, which unites the entire world into a single market system. On the other hand, there is 'a process of fragmentation into closed identities, and the culturalist and relativist ideology that accompanies this fragmentation' – in other words, identity politics and ethnic conflicts.[43] Although they initially seem contradictory, Badiou argues, 'The capitalist logic of the general equivalent and the identitarian and cultural logic of communities or minorities form an articulated whole.'[44] Various identity groups provide market niches, and more importantly, ethnic and national differences allow workers to be divided against each other, as when the use of cheaper labour in a 'developing' country depresses wages or reduces the number of jobs in the same industry in a more 'advanced' country. With this frame in mind, Žižek begins *The Fragile Absolute* with a discussion of racism, set in terms of the ethnic conflicts in the Balkans and Western attitudes toward those conflicts, moving on from there to an analysis of contemporary capitalism. *On Belief* is couched in terms of what has been Žižek's corollary to the critique of nationalism and racism since *Tarrying with the Negative*: harsh denunciation of liberals.

In both cases, the connection between Žižek's analysis of the contemporary situation and a specifically Pauline intervention is left largely implicit. *The Puppet and the Dwarf* clarifies this connection, in a way that also ties Paul more closely to Žižek's system, by focusing on what he takes to be the problem Paul is dealing with in Romans 7: the temptation of *perversion*. For Žižek, contemporary society is increasingly characterized by perversion. As capitalism takes on ever-new forms and generates ever-new desires, it tends to break down the subjective structures that served as the objects of 'classic' psychoanalysis: namely, hysterical and obsessional neurosis. In place of these complex and ambiguous stances toward the law and its superego supplement, more and more people identify directly with the superego injunction to enjoy. Žižek discusses this in terms of a general culture of hedonism. On the one hand, subjects increasingly think of themselves as consumers and view their choices among various consumer goods as the field in which they can best assert their identity. On the other hand, traditional moral rules are replaced by a concern for 'health', which for Žižek means primarily an attempt to make sure that enjoyment does not get out of hand and become self-destructive. A major symptom of this latter tendency is the series of products that have had their harmful element removed – decaffeinated coffee, diet soda, light beer, fat-free ice cream, etc. – which have often figured prominently in Žižek's public lectures. These health concerns are only one example of a structural principle of perversion: what the pervert fundamentally wants is

The Christian experience

not unfettered enjoyment, but the imposition of a law that will help to keep enjoyment at a manageable level.

What has caused this widespread perversion? For Žižek, the cause is ultimately the advent of modernity, which has permanently undercut the 'big Other' of tradition. If past societies could regard themselves as based in God's will or the natural order of things, modernity is the society for which 'God is dead', or in psychoanalytic terms, 'the big Other doesn't exist'. The social edifice obviously didn't collapse in one fell swoop, but as a result of the 'death of God', the modern subject experiences at least some minimal distance from his or her social role – one can take on the role of parent, or child, or professional, or labourer, but forever lost is the sense that one immediately *is* that role. This minimal distance is the reason that Žižek is able to say that the subject as empty self-relating negativity or 'vanishing mediator' is the most fundamental form of modern subjectivity. This situation seems obviously preferable to ancient systems in which even the most enlightened philosophers (most notably Aristotle) could believe that certain people were simply born to be slaves. At the same time, freedom is hugely anxiety-producing. This anxiety is visible on an everyday level. Žižek frequently uses the example of romantic love: in the absence of clear rules for courtship, people have no way to know in advance whether their attempts at seduction will be regarded as appropriate or else experienced as 'harassment'. One could also get at this problem by imagining the absence of a convention that arguably still is in force. For instance, what if the ritual of shaking hands were no longer the dominant mode of introducing oneself? Even now, at least in my social circles, it's unclear whether a handshake is strictly required, but what if it became potentially offensive for certain people – even as others regarded the lack of a handshake as offensive? In the face of this ambiguity, meeting someone new would suddenly become much more anxiety-producing than it already naturally is.

As discussed in the first chapter, the big Other serves both to shield the subject from the raw destructive force of *jouissance* and to provide a modicum of *jouissance* through the law's inherent transgression. The 'death of God' or 'non-existence of the big Other' therefore puts the subject in a double-bind. On the one hand, without the law, *jouissance* threatens to overwhelm the subject. On the other hand, the breakdown of the law also threatens to deprive the subject of the little bits of *jouissance* the subject derives from transgressing the law. Perversion is an attempt to deal with this double-bind:

> Perversion is a double strategy to counteract this nonexistence [of the big Other]: an (ultimately deeply conservative, nostalgic) attempt to install the law artificially, *in the desperate hope that we will then take this self-posited limitation 'seriously'*, and, in a complementary way, a no less desperate attempt to codify the very transgression of the Law . . .[45]

In the context of the culture of hedonism, then, the imposition of 'traditional values' is not a solution, but rather a way of intensifying the problem. The phenomenon of the 'religious right' in the United States provides a particularly vivid example of this feedback loop. On the surface, the attempt to impose 'traditional values' represents an attempt to suppress *jouissance*, but the 'religious right' position is actually sustained by an 'ambiguous attitude of horror/envy with regard to the unspeakable pleasures in which sinners engage'.[46] Even setting aside the numerous sex scandals involving major religious right figures, this fascination with sinful *jouissance* is clearly shown in former Republican senator Rick Santorum's infamous remarks claiming that the acceptance of homosexuality will lead inevitably to acceptance of 'man on dog' sex.[47] Only an obsession with transgressive sexuality would make such a connection seem plausible – and lest Santorum appear to be an isolated case, I should point out that similar reasoning can be found in Supreme Court Justice Antonin Scalia's dissent in the *Lawrence v. Texas* ruling, which struck down state sodomy laws.

Recent shifts in rhetorical strategies on the religious right demonstrate the inherent instability of this strategy of perversion: now it is claimed that following traditional moral values by remaining a virgin until marriage will actually lead to a better sex life in the long run. Leaving aside the question of the empirical accuracy of such claims, this approach of instrumentalizing traditional values in the service of sex renders those values ultimately dispensable. If the admitted goal is having a satisfying sex life, what

The Christian experience

stands in the way of casting traditional morality aside if it fails to deliver? At that point, of course, the subject is faced once again with the anxiety that led to the reimposition of 'tradition' in the first place.

At its most extreme, the anxiety attendant on the 'death of God' leaves us susceptible to the totalitarian temptation.[48] This problem is not limited to religious fundamentalists – it is the key experience of the modern West. Heidegger's involvement with Nazism provides perhaps the most notorious example of a major thinker succumbing to the totalitarian temptation, but Žižek concedes that a tendency toward perversion can be found even in Lacan.[49] Since the double-bind of perversion is a characteristically Western problem, one possible way to escape it might be to turn toward Eastern religions. Žižek rejects this option, focusing his analysis on the Eastern religion that is most admired by Westerners: Buddhism. As noted at the beginning of this chapter, Žižek initially shows a certain admiration for Buddhism in *The Fragile Absolute*,[50] but his view becomes increasingly negative. In *The Puppet and the Dwarf* and elsewhere, he argues that Western Buddhism serves only to help subjects to adapt to the extreme demands of contemporary capitalism. He then takes a step further, critiquing Zen Buddhism as underwriting militarism in Japan and other societies.[51] Clearly turning East is not the solution for Žižek.

Given that he presents Paul's argument in Romans 7 as geared toward escaping perversion, then, one might reasonably expect Žižek to claim that the only option is to return to an authentically Christian position. Indeed, in his chapter on G. K. Chesterton,[52] he initially appears to be doing precisely that, using Chesterton's *Orthodoxy* as representative of the Christian stance and injecting his insights directly into contemporary debates that show a certain perverse logic, such as upholding liberal democratic values through torture.[53] Yet despite his obvious respect for Chesterton's writing style – as evidenced by the unusually high number of block-quotes – and generally Hegelian style of thought, Žižek's ultimate goal in this chapter is to demonstrate that perversion is actually the key strategy of 'really existing Christianity'.[54] Chesterton's position, at bottom, is the same as that of contemporary evangelicals who promise better sex through traditional morality: 'Christianity is the only frame for pagan freedom.'[55] In other words, the Christian system of prohibitions and self-denial 'is the only frame within which we can enjoy pagan pleasures: the feeling of guilt is a fake enabling us to give ourselves over to pleasures [. . .]'.[56] Žižek comes to a similar conclusion about Richard Wagner, another figure he deeply admires, but whose opera *Parsifal*, with its narrative of redemptive suffering, demonstrates that 'the ultimate fake of Christianity is that it sustains its official message of inner peace and redemption by a morbid excitation, namely, a fixation on the suffering, mutilated corpse of Christ'.[57]

In fact, Žižek goes so far as to wonder if the Christian God himself is a pervert, in that he seems to *need* the Fall to occur in order to be able to redeem humanity and to *need* Judas to commit the despicable act of betraying Jesus in order to carry out his plan of redemption. This moment of perversion, where God himself seems to operate according to the principle, 'Let us do evil that good may result', is the 'perverse core of Christianity' referred to in the subtitle of *The Puppet and the Dwarf*.[58] The only way to get at the revolutionary potential of Christianity's founding gesture is to jettison this perverse core – and the first necessary step is to fully grasp the distinctiveness of the Jewish context in which Pauline Christianity arose.

Job and Judaism

Over the course of his three books on Christianity, Žižek's esteem for Judaism steadily grows. Already in his somewhat ambiguous stance in *The Fragile Absolute*, however, Žižek has departed significantly from Badiou's position. In *Saint Paul*, Badiou casts Judaism as a perpetual foil, summing up all the qualities that Paul's mission opposes. Where Paul has a universal message, Judaism is resolutely particular; where Paul preaches grace, Judaism relies on the law; and ultimately, where Paul opens the door to authentic life, the Jewish law is the path of death.[59] Although he stridently rejects the anti-Semitic claim that the Jews are to blame for Christ's crucifixion, in his stance toward the law Badiou stands in a long Christian tradition of anti-Judaism, and in fact he even appears to go beyond that tradition, claiming in an aside that the inclusion of the commandment 'love your neighbour as yourself' in the Old

Testament amounts to little more than a coincidence, albeit one that is politically convenient for Paul's mission.[60] As noted above, the root of this negative evaluation of the Jewish law is what Badiou calls 'death drive' and Žižek calls the 'obscene superego supplement'. Yet despite his evolving position, one point in Žižek's theorization of Judaism is constant: the Jewish stance toward the law is (uniquely) free of the logic of the superego or 'inherent transgression'. What is not constant is his reason *why* this is the case.

In *The Fragile Absolute* and (perhaps to a lesser extent) *On Belief*, Žižek attempts to ground his understanding of Judaism in Freud's *Moses and Monotheism*.[61] In this strange and complicated work, Freud sets out his theory that Moses was an Egyptian who adhered to the worship of Aton, the first recorded instance of monotheism. When the pharaoh who had imposed Aton-worship on Egypt was deposed, Moses turned to the Jewish slaves and led them out of Egypt in the hope of perpetuating the religion of Aton. Moses proved to be an overly harsh leader, however, and so 'the Jews, who even according to the Bible were stubborn and unruly towards their lawgiver and leader, rebelled at last, killed him, and threw off the imposed Aton religion as the Egyptians had done before them'.[62] Just as the murdered primal father in *Totem and Taboo* is transformed into a domineering internalized authority by his guilty sons, the murdered Moses returned in a more fearsome and powerful form, namely that of Yahweh. Freud argues that Paul's 'creation of a new religion' based on the death of Christ was an attempt to move beyond this primal crime through a kind of short-circuit.[63] Christianity's message to the Jews as to all other religions is, 'You won't *admit* that you murdered God', which is to say 'the archetype of God, the primeval Father, and his reincarnations.' Christians, by contrast, can say, 'It is true, we did the same thing, but we *admitted* it, and since then we have been purified.'[64]

Žižek's initial attempts to use Freud's myth lead to significant contradictions. One particularly clear example is found in *On Belief*. There Žižek claims that Jewish subjects '*only* stick to the *symbolic rules*, deprived of the obscene fantasmatic background. There is no place in Judaism for the private wink of understanding, no obscene solidarity about their shared complicity among the perpetrators of the transgression.'[65] Later, however, citing Eric

89

Santner, he claims that 'Judaism is a religion whose public discourse is haunted by the spectral shadow of its obscene uncanny double, of its excessive transgressive founding violent gesture (it is this very disavowed attachment to the traumatic kernel which confers on Judaism its extraordinary chutzpah and durability) [. . .].'[66] The 'transgressive founding violent gesture' of course refers to Freud's account of the murder of Moses. The first contradiction to note, then, is that in Freud's theory, *every* community is grounded in some disavowed founding crime – thus the Jews' founding crime cannot in itself account for their uniqueness as a nation, whether in terms of 'chutzpah' or otherwise. More specifically, the structure of internalized authority that Freud describes in *Totem and Taboo* and *Moses and Monotheism* is precisely what *generates* the superego, so even if the founding crime of the Jewish community were somehow the source of the uniqueness of the Jewish nation, it could not be the source for the specific form of uniqueness Žižek claims, namely, a lack of superego.

By the time he comes to write *The Puppet and the Dwarf*, Žižek has essentially given up on the attempt to explain the uniqueness of the Jewish nation directly in Freud's terms. Rather than reject Freud's theory, however, Žižek supplements it. Freud's theory still serves to explain the emergence of the Jews as a particular ethnic group,[67] but to account for the distinctiveness that he sees in the Jewish stance toward the law – and ultimately to ground his most systematic stance on Christianity – Žižek develops his own account of Jewish origins. Instead of focusing on obvious alternative founders like Abraham or King David, however, Žižek turns to a more exceptional figure within the Jewish tradition: Job. In contrast with the masculine 'master' figures like Moses or David, Job here represents the hysterical questioning that Žižek elsewhere argues is the absolutely necessary first step toward revolutionary change:

> What makes the Book of Job so provocative is not simply the presence of multiple perspectives without a clear resolution [. . .]; Job's perplexity stems from the fact that he experiences God as an impenetrable Thing; he is uncertain what He wants from him in inflicting the ordeals to which he is submitted [. . .], and consequently, he – Job – is

unable to ascertain how he fits into the overall divine order, unable to recognize his place in it.[68]

As is well known, at the end of the book God finally intervenes into the conversation, but doesn't provide any direct answer. Instead, one finds 'a God who acts like someone caught in a moment of impotence – or, at the very least, weakness – and tries to escape His predicament by empty boasting'.[69]

Job is able to bring God to this extreme point through the very relentlessness of his questioning. Žižek dismisses the popular image of Job as 'a patient sufferer, enduring his ordeal with a firm faith in God – on the contrary, he complains all the time, rejecting his fate [. . .]' and insisting on 'the utter *meaninglessness* of his suffering'. This uncompromising stance qualifies the Book of Job as 'the first exemplary case of the critique of ideology in human history, laying bare the basic discursive strategies of legitimizing suffering' through his debate with his 'theologian' friends. Ultimately, even God cannot resist and 'takes [Job's] side at the end, claiming that every word Job spoke was true, while every word the three theologians spoke was false'.[70] God's admission that Job was in the right dovetails with his impotent 'acting-out' in response to Job's challenge, but instead of taking the next step and openly declaring that God has failed him, Job remains silent. Žižek argues that Job chooses this route

> neither because he was crushed by God's overwhelming presence, nor because he wanted thereby to indicate his continuous resistance, that is, the fact that God avoided answering Job's question, but because, in a gesture of silent solidarity, he perceived the divine impotence. God is neither just nor unjust, simply impotent. What Job suddenly understood was that it *was not him, but God Himself, who was actually on trial in Job's calamities*, and He failed the test miserably.[71]

This encounter with the divine impotence is what sets the Jews apart from every other nation.

For Žižek, the Jewish community still has something analogous to a superego structure – Job's silence represents the fact that the

Jewish community chooses to continue to 'keep up appearances', and so Jewish group identity is still formed in reference to a disavowed trauma or 'spectral narrative'. Nevertheless, the Jewish structure is ultimately unique:

> A crucial line of separation is to be drawn here between the Jewish fidelity to the disavowed ghosts and the pagan obscene initiatory wisdom accompanying public ritual: the disavowed Jewish spectral narrative does not tell the obscene story of God's impenetrable omnipotence, but its exact opposite: the story of His *impotence* concealed by the standard pagan obscene supplements.[72]

This fundamental difference corresponds to the more obvious difference between the Jews and other ethnic communities: their remarkable resilience and continuity, despite so many centuries as a diaspora community. Though Žižek does not make this connection explicit, one could say that when a 'normal' ethnic group experiences the impotence of their God in the form of some kind of catastrophe, it undermines the group identity, in some cases even causing them to disappear as a distinct group. By contrast, the Jewish community is directly founded on that divine impotence, accounting for its 'unprecedented vitality'.[73]

The unique Jewish stance toward the law is in turn grounded in the Jews' lack of a proper place among nations. Citing Eric Santner's *On the Psychotheology of Everyday Life*,[74] Žižek argues that the Jewish law 'relies on a gesture of "unplugging": by means of reference to the Law, Jews in diaspora maintain a distance toward the society in which they live'. Accordingly, the Jewish law is different from all other systems of law: 'while other (pagan) laws regulate social exchange, the Jewish Law introduces a different dimension, that of divine justice which is radically heterogeneous with regard to the social law'. In terms of Freud's *Totem and Taboo*, all (pagan) societies are founded on the fantasy of an omnipotent father-figure (or God) with access to unfettered *jouissance*, and the corresponding notion of justice is ultimately a 'reestablished balance' tantamount to 'the victorious reassertion of the right/might of the Whole over its parts' – in other words, a reassertion of the ideological fantasy that legitimates the injustices at the heart of any society. By contrast, the Jewish conception of justice is 'the vision of the final state in which all the wrongs done to individuals will be undone'.[75] This concept of justice is a standing rebuke to the ideological fantasy, which is what one would expect from a nation whose representative figure, Job, is for Žižek the first critic of ideology. For this reason, Žižek can later say in *The Parallax View*: 'the proclamation of the Decalogue is not a normal case of ideological interpellation: the Decalogue is precisely a law *deprived* of the obscene fantasmatic support'.[76] Any attempt to escape from the perverse logic of the 'obscene superego supplement', therefore, must begin here.

Cross and collective

For Žižek, Paul's revolutionary gesture can only be properly understood in light of its Jewish context. In this respect, Žižek is in agreement with the general consensus of biblical scholars, who have increasingly argued in favour of a Jewish Paul. More than that, in line with those scholars who argue with Krister Stendahl that Paul did not view himself as a convert,[77] Žižek claims that 'Paul did not simply pass from the Jewish position to another position, he did something with, within, and to the Jewish position itself.'[78] Furthermore, in line with Stendahl, Paul's change of position is most fundamentally 'a new understanding of the law which is otherwise an obstacle to the Gentiles'.[79] Perhaps the best way to get at Žižek's understanding of the precise obstacle the law poses for Gentiles is through what seems to me to be a surface-level contradiction, but a very revealing one, in his interpretation of Romans 7.

Following an almost unbroken historical tradition, Žižek claims that the Jewish law is 'the main target of Paul's critique' in Romans 7[80] – that is to say, Paul believes that the Jewish law is based on the logic of the 'obscene superego supplement' that ultimately leads to the temptation of perversion. Yet for Žižek, the Jewish law 'is already a law deprived of its superego supplement, not relying on any obscene support'. Remarkably, then, Žižek ends up *defending* the Jewish law against Paul's supposed attack in Romans 7, arguing that *both* Judaism and Christianity escape the perverse 'pagan' law that feeds off of its own inherent transgression. The problem with this position is obvious: it presupposes that Žižek understands the Jewish law better than Paul does. If forced to resolve this contradiction, Žižek (it seems to me) would almost certainly give up the idea that Paul's main target is the Jewish law, simply because he hangs no further interpretative weight on it whatsoever. In so doing, he would again bring himself into line with Stendahl, who points out that in Paul's writings, 'there is no indication that he had had any difficulty in fulfilling the Law' and therefore argues Romans 7 cannot be read as an account of Paul's own inner struggle[81] – and also in line with Origen, the first commentator on Romans, who claims that the spiritual life would be a hopeless pursuit if Paul were speaking of himself in Romans 7.[82]

In contrast, then, with the traditional reading of Romans 7, Žižek claims that the Jewish stance toward the law is not the problem, but precisely the solution. Paul's achievement is to bring Gentiles also into the Jewish 'unplugged' stance toward the law, allowing them to 'suspend the obscene libidinal investment in the Law, the investment on account of which the Law generates/solicits its own transgression'.[83] In explaining how Paul manages to do this, Žižek echoes Freud's basic scheme of the relationship between Judaism and Christianity, namely, his contention that Paul founds Christianity by revealing what Judaism kept hidden. Yet where Freud views Christ as a repetition of Moses, Žižek views him as a repetition – and radicalization – of Job. As discussed above, Job perceives the divine impotence behind God's blustery display of power, but chooses to remain silent out of solidarity with that impotence. In this way, Job maintains the logic of the 'subject supposed to believe', keeping up appearances for the sake of the big Other, which here represents not God, but the human 'public' in general. One good example of this logic is the adult stance toward Santa Claus. Everyone plays along, professing belief in Santa Claus so as not to disturb the children's presumed naïve belief – and the true Žižekian twist comes when the children are old enough to have figured out the ruse, but continue to act as though they believe so as not to undermine the *parents'* belief in the innocent belief of their children.

Christ breaks this cycle of the 'subject supposed to believe' through his cry of dereliction on the cross. Here, just as in his argument that the radicality of Schelling's thought is only accessible if one *preserves* the theological trappings, Žižek insists on preserving the traditional view of Christ as the incarnation of God. If Christ were 'demythologized' as merely one prophet among others, he would be little more than another Job, though a Job deprived of God's boastful non-answer. Yet because Christ *is* God, his cry of dereliction has much more radical consequences: in Chesterton's words, on the cross, 'God seemed for an instant to be an atheist.'[84] Paul's preaching of the cross is therefore more than simply the equivalent of the cynical child who points out to his comrades that Santa Claus doesn't exist – what Paul reveals is that *God* has faced up to his own impotence.

For Žižek, Paul's true genius lies in his perception that God's self-abandonment on the cross is actually the best possible news. As early as *For They Know Not*, Žižek held up this gesture as the ultimate example of a dialectical 'negation of negation', a change in perspective that transforms an apparent defeat into the greatest victory.[85] The theological word for this triumph is of course the resurrection. In line with Hegel, Žižek interprets the resurrection as ultimately identical with the advent of the Holy Spirit, here understood as the bond of the new community founded on Christ. Like the Jewish community, the Pauline community is bound together by solidarity with the impotence of God or the big Other, meaning that it shares the Jewish 'unplugged' stance toward the law, free of the obscene superego supplement. Žižek explains this 'unplugging' in terms of Paul's logic of the 'as if not', found in 1 Corinthians:

> I mean, brothers and sisters, the appointed time has grown short; from now on, let even those who have wives be as though they had none, and those who mourn as though they were not mourning, and those who rejoice as though they were not rejoicing, and those who buy as though they had no possessions, and those who deal with the world as though they had no dealings with it. For the present form of this world is passing away.[86]

One must not mistake this 'as if not' attitude for the cynical distance that every ideology cultivates and that leaves the ideological fantasy intact. Instead, Paul is here describing 'the disavowal of the symbolic realm itself: I use symbolic obligations, but I am not performatively *bound* by them'.[87] In other words, the Pauline subject escapes the logic of 'surplus obedience' through which *jouissance* binds the subject to the law.

What distinguishes this new community from the Jewish community is that it dispenses with the secret 'spectral narrative': 'The secret to which the Jews remain faithful is the horror of the divine impotence – and it is *this* secret that is "revealed" in Christianity. This is why Christianity could occur only after Judaism: it reveals the horror first confronted by the Jews.'[88] By virtue of being founded on the public revelation of the impotence of the big Other, the Pauline community 'provides the first example of a collective that is not formed and held together through the mechanism described by Freud in *Totem and Taboo* and *Moses and Monotheism* [. . .]'.[89] The significance of this new type of community is twofold. First, it represents the first form of sociality that is truly *universal*, in the sense that 'I can participate in this universal dimension [of the Holy Spirit] *directly*, irrespective of my special place within the global social order',[90] or as Paul puts it: 'There is no longer Jew or Greek, there is no longer slave or free, there is no longer male and female; for all of you are one in Christ Jesus.'[91] Second, and correlatively, the Pauline community is the first form of sociality without any hidden subtext to supplement the 'official' public face. For Žižek, the formation of this type of sociality is ultimately the goal of psychoanalysis, which seeks 'to practice a language which *does not deceive* or conceal'[92] – the opposite of the perverse stance of violating the law in order to preserve it or 'doing evil that good may result'.

Love beyond the law

Thus far I have only described the 'Holy Spirit' as a new form of sociality in negative terms: a universality that embraces difference, an 'unplugged' stance toward the law. In many respects, such a social practice might sound similar to the 'liberal tolerance', with its attendant cynical distance, that Žižek so stridently critiques. The key difference is that whereas 'liberal tolerance' takes up (in theory at least) a purely negative stance of abstracting from differences such as race, religion, gender, etc., according everyone a generic set of human rights, Christian love goes beyond the 'official' surface-level particularities to the *absolute* particularity of *objet petit a*. This distinctive form of love is 'intolerant' and even 'violent', continually cutting below the subject's symbolic identity to get at the *jouissance* that sustains him or her. In line with the Christian tradition, and particularly the tradition stemming from Augustine's meditations on the Trinity, Žižek identifies the Holy Spirit with this bond of love – but, in contradiction with traditional Christianity, he identifies the Holy Spirit as the immediate consequence of the crucifixion as the 'death of God' or public revelation of the impotence of the big Other. That is to say, the Holy Spirit as the bond of love is dialectically identical to the 'death of God', bodying forth the negativity of the cross.

Žižek can say this because of his distinctive Christology. In orthodox Christology, the second person (hypostasis) of the Trinity assumes human nature, which one naturally tends to think of as a kind of positive 'something' added on to the divine nature. Žižek takes this basic scheme and adds a dialectical twist. From the point of view of the divine, Christ's humanity is a necessary 'fallout' of a gap within God himself, which Žižek discusses in terms of the impotence of God encountered by Job – that is, the incarnation is a kind of radicalization of God's identification with Job. From the point of view of the human, Christ's divinity is ultimately the gap that separates him from other human beings, a gap that is most clearly displayed in his suffering and death on the cross. As an outcast, however, Christ embodies humanity as such – in line with the Pauline claim, taken up by later theologians ranging from Irenaeus to Reinhold Niebuhr, that Christ is the 'second Adam', repeating or recapitulating Adam (who is the representative of all of humanity) in order to redeem humanity. For Žižek, however, this redemption must be thought as a kind of setting humanity free *from* God, rather than the traditional notion of settling our account with God so as to be entitled to heavenly reward: '. . . after [Christ's] death, there is no place for any God of Beyond: all that remains is the Holy Spirit, the community of believers onto which the unfathomable aura of Christ passes once it is deprived of its bodily incarnation'.[93]

Christ as the self-undermining 'big Other' opens up the possibility of a collective of subjects who are directly confronted with each other's *jouissance* – that is, a collectivity founded on the Real of the subject rather than on the symbolic fiction. In contrast with sentimental forms of love that idealize the other subject, Christian love directly identifies with the finitude and weakness of the other subject, just as Christian theology identifies a despised outcast directly with God himself. Žižek identifies the underlying logic of the 'Holy Spirit' with the 'discourse of the analyst', in which every subject has undergone 'subjective destitution', identifying with *objet petit a* – a sociality that is itself opened up by the analyst's role as a paradoxically self-undermining big Other. Finally, given that the ultimate goal of Žižek's reworking of the concept of a truth-event is *political*, Žižek also draws a parallel between the 'Holy Spirit' or 'discourse of the analyst' and the authentic revolutionary collective, for which Lenin's Bolshevik revolution serves as his primary reference point. Thus the notion of a different, non-ideological social bond is not purely utopian in the sense of being a mere ideal for the future – for Žižek, such a thing really has broken out before in history: Paul really did establish collectives based in the unique form of love called the 'Holy Spirit', Lacan really did struggle to form a collective of analysts, Lenin really did lead a genuine revolution, and (though he does not explicitly mention it in this context) Eastern European activists really did participate in an authentically non-ideological movement when they undermined Communism.

Yet this new form of collectivity is inherently fragile. Lenin's revolution led to the imposition of Stalinism, which for Žižek is the quintessential form of perversion. In *The Puppet and the Dwarf*, Žižek draws continual analogies between 'really existing Christianity' and Stalinism, arguing that Paul's collectives eventually declined into perversion as well. This turn to perversion happened when the very things that were intended to pull Gentiles out of the pagan stance toward law – the idea of Christ as the sacrifice that abolishes the order of sacrifice,[94] the notion of 'love beyond the law' and forgiveness of sins[95] – ended up being turned back on themselves, leading Christians to return to paganism. The notion of mercy and forgiveness thus became yet another 'wink and nudge' from authority, providing a release valve of transgressive *jouissance*, and within the pagan view of law, Christ's sacrifice becomes an insurmountable debt, binding the subject instead of setting her free. This happened because Christianity ultimately rejected the Jewish stance toward law, which was the only way to gain access to the specifically Christian dimension of love. Without the Jewish stance, its unique form of universal love collapsed in on itself – and so Christian anti-Semitism ultimately testifies to the fact that by rejecting the Jewish experience, Christianity has transformed its subversive kernel into its 'perverse core'.

In order to jettison that 'perverse core', Christianity must return to its founding moment as the 'religion of atheism', the religion in which even God is an atheist. Perversion is an identification with the obscene *jouissance* that underwrites the authority of the big Other, but the authentic gesture of Christianity is acknowledging the non-existence of the big Other: 'When Christ dies, what dies with him is the secret hope discernible in "Father, why hast thou forsaken me?": the hope that there *is* a father who has abandoned me. The "Holy Spirit" [as the new kind of social bond that arises in Christ's death] is the community deprived of its support in the big Other.' Thus Žižek's goal in turning to the Christian tradition is not so much to reclaim religion as to combat 'the religious hard core that survives even in humanism, even up to Stalinism, with its belief in History as the "big Other" that decides on the "objective meaning" of our deeds'. For Christianity to regain its subversive kernel today, therefore, it must take the risk of an authentic Žižekian ethical act, in the sense of a self-directed choice of the worst, by 'abandoning the shell of its institutional organization (and, even more so, of its specific religious experience)'.[96] Such a move would be in line with the Benjaminian concept of revolution discussed at the beginning of this chapter: reaching back into the past to redeem a potential that was defeated.

Žižek's prescription for contemporary Christianity will perhaps be discouraging for some, but it makes sense in light of the claim that 'to become a true dialectical materialist, one should go through the Christian experience', and its necessary correlative, namely, that Christianity's subversive 'kernel is accessible *only* to a materialist approach'.[97] This subversive kernel is not simply the negative gesture of atheism, but the new bond of distinctively Christian love – a love that is necessarily 'materialist', addressing itself to the *jouissance* at the core of the other subject. The philosophy of dialectical materialism, then, does not treat the Christian experience as a dispensable preface, but maintains the materialist bond of love opened up by Christ's death on the cross as its motivating force – which in practice means that the 'other side' of the Christian experience is itself articulated in theological terms and continues to address core theological issues. It is to this theological materialism that I turn in the next chapter.

Chapter 4

Dialectical materialism, or the philosophy of freedom

This chapter rounds out my exposition of Žižek's intellectual trajectory with a discussion of the necessary corollary of his account of 'the Christian experience': dialectical materialism. As indicated at the end of the last chapter, 'the Christian experience' is more than a disposable example or a preamble to Žižek's development of dialectical materialism. *The Parallax View* (2006) not only carries forward the major conclusions of his reading of Christianity as established in *The Puppet and the Dwarf*, thereby integrating his work on Christianity into his project as a whole, but also couches new developments in theological terms and includes explicit discussions of theology in short passages and, most notably, in an extended discussion of Kierkegaard. Beyond that, his key concerns at this stage are shared with the theological tradition: first of all the reality of human freedom. In practice, of course, the question of 'free will vs. predestination', Arminians vs. Calvinists, seems to have been decided in favour of the Arminians more or less by default, as fewer and fewer theologians or laypeople embrace the rather grim teaching of double predestination. At the same time, certain developments in twentieth-century theology indicate that this instinctive embrace of a genuine human freedom has not always been convincingly grounded intellectually – opening the door for process theology, which attempts to ground the reality of God and human freedom in the metaphysics of Alfred North Whitehead, and the more popularized 'open theism' movement, which posits a finite God so as to 'make room' for human free will.

Žižek's solution to the problem of freedom is more akin to process theology's, or at least Whitehead's, insofar as he attempts to ground freedom directly in the physical sciences.[1] Žižek's ambitions in this regard can be seen in the final section of *The Indivisible Remainder*, entitled 'Quantum Physics With Lacan', where he develops an analogy between the rise of the big Other out of the mutual incomprehension of human subjects and the rise of the familiar world of Newtonian mechanics out of the paradoxical and mysterious realm of quantum physics. Žižek's subsequent works in the 'middle' phase, however, do not follow up on the claims in that final section: *Plague of Fantasies* primarily develops his theory of ideology critique in relation to the category of fantasy, *Ticklish Subject* advances his theory of 'Cartesian subjectivity' against what he takes to be widespread misunderstanding about the true meaning of Descartes' gesture, and his three books on Christianity serve as a way of moving forward his ethical and political thought. In *The Parallax View*, however, the concept of 'dialectical materialism' becomes the structuring principle of his project, and whatever tentativeness may have been present in the final section of *The Indivisible Remainder* has disappeared – indeed, Žižek goes far beyond a modest claim that his thought is in harmony with science, arguing that his philosophical materialism can actually intervene into the scientific field (specifically cognitive science) in order to help resolve its deadlocks and inconsistencies. Though his end result is significantly different from Whitehead's – most notably, in the present context, Žižek does not end up affirming a concept of God, at least not in quite the same way – his gesture is essentially the same: replacing an outdated, though at this point instinctive, metaphysical system with one that can really make sense of the latest science and simultaneously do justice to the experience of human freedom.

The bulk of this chapter will be taken up with an exposition of the notion of dialectical materialism and Žižek's engagement with the sciences – quantum mechanics, cognitive science, and evolutionary theory. The latter in particular will provide an occasion to explain the crucial concept of the 'death drive' in greater detail. Along the way, I will make reference to the more or less standard 'God of the gaps' approach to the relationship between theology and science and to Žižek's attempt to give a 'theological' grounding to the project of modern science. I will conclude my account of Žižek's use of science with a comparison between Žižek's approach and Wolfhart Pannenberg's proposal for a theological intervention in the human sciences. Having established the overall scheme, I will then turn to two topics that, for the Christian tradition as for Žižek, are inextricably tied with the notion of

Dialectical materialism, or the philosophy of freedom

human freedom. First, I will address Žižek's account of the ethics that correspond to dialectical materialism, a discussion that Žižek situates within an extended critical reading of Kierkegaard. His reading of Kierkegaard also serves as an opportunity to clarify the role of theology within his system. Finally, I will conclude with a consideration of the political reflections with which Žižek ends *The Parallax View*, where he carries forward his notion of the 'Holy Spirit' or 'discourse of the analyst' as a model for a liberative political practice. Overall, then, this chapter, though dealing with 'materialism', is nonetheless one of the most straightforwardly 'theological' in this book.

What is dialectical materialism?

In order to understand what Žižek means by 'dialectical materialism', it is helpful to have some grasp on the standard, non-dialectical materialism, sometimes called 'vulgar' materialism. This type of materialism takes the methods of the physical sciences as a model for epistemology or the theory of knowledge. The first premise is that matter is the only thing that is real and that all matter behaves in accordance with certain laws. Since physical law is inescapable, the general assumption among materialists is that the universe is *deterministic* – that is, in principle, every event is completely predictable. Our inability to predict every event stems from our ignorance of the full range of causes contributing to it. Yet we do know that large-scale phenomena ultimately stem from the complex interactions of the most basic constituents of matter, in accordance with fundamental physical laws. While scientists seldom take this logic to the extreme – for instance, trying to explain the behaviour of a bird by direct reference to the interactions of the atoms that make it up – the general tendency is toward *reductionism*, meaning that a complex phenomenon can be best understood by first reducing it to more basic processes.

No one can deny that the physical sciences are an extremely powerful and successful method of acquiring knowledge about, and thereby control over, the world. Nevertheless, as a philosophical stance, 'vulgar' materialism runs into trouble when it comes to explaining specifically human phenomena. On the one hand, in a purely deterministic universe, there is no room for human freedom as we intuitively experience it. On the other hand, in a reductionist approach, it is difficult to see our experience of an autonomous realm of consciousness or thought as anything other than an illusion – our thoughts are 'really' neurons firing, our emotions are 'really' chemical imbalances, etc. In a true triumph of understatement, the attempt to reconcile 'vulgar' materialism with our experience of freedom and consciousness is therefore widely known as 'the hard question'.

One way to get out of this bind is to claim that the realm of determinism is not all there is. God, for example, or the soul is able to intervene in the physical realm without being determined by it. In order to have any credibility, this approach must be able to demonstrate that it has genuine explanatory power, and the standard way to achieve this is to argue that science faces insoluble problems that only a supernatural explanation can unravel. The most prominent current example of an attempt to interject supernatural explanation into science is 'intelligent design', which claims that there are holes in the theory of evolution that only the intervention of an intelligent designer can fill. One standard argument is that some biological phenomena are 'irreducibly complex', meaning that they could only have come into existence all at once, as opposed to the piecewise manner that evolution requires. The problem with this 'God of the gaps' approach is that the progress of science has left progressively fewer 'gaps' for God to fill – for example, scientists were already able to answer the question of 'irreducible complexity' even before the intelligent design movement arose. Instead of contributing to scientific knowledge, therefore, the 'God of the gaps' approach has consistently been on the defensive, further and further reducing the role of the supernatural as science deprives it of more and more footholds.

In terms of Lacan's formulae of sexuation discussed in Chapter 2, the 'God of the gaps' approach corresponds to the 'masculine' logic of the constitutive exception – that is, it posits an entity outside the realm of determinism that nonetheless is necessary to found it and give it consistency. Žižek's approach follows the 'feminine' logic, showing again that the hyphen makes all the difference: it's not that the realm of determinism is 'not all' there is, in the sense that something escapes it, but rather that the realm of determinism is 'non-all', meaning inherently non-totalized or

Dialectical materialism, or the philosophy of freedom

non-saturated. This 'leaves room', not for positive entities like God or the soul, but for nothingness or negativity – most notably subjectivity, which for Žižek is not a substance on the model of Descartes' *res cogitans* or thinking thing, but a self-relating negativity. These instances of negativity can intervene in the non-all realm of positive being and have real effects, meaning that dialectical materialism is 'by definition nonreductionist: far from claiming that "everything is matter", it confers upon "immaterial" phenomena a specific positive nonbeing'.[2] More generally, this positive role of negativity means that each successive 'level' of reality has its own relative autonomy. In the example Žižek focuses on in *The Indivisible Remainder*, for instance, the big Other arises out of the interactions among subjects, but its very ability to function depends on every subject taking up a negative stance toward it, that is, experiencing themselves as alienated from a social order that exists over against them. The big Other positively embodies the lack of common ground among subjects, serving as a virtual symbolic order that nonetheless has real effects.

If dialectical materialism were *simply* non-reductive, then it would be difficult to distinguish it from metaphysical schemes that directly posit non-material beings. It distinguishes itself from such schemes insofar as it is *dialectical*, meaning that successive 'levels' emerge out of the inherent conflicts and deadlocks within the previous level. To stay with the same example, the big Other as a virtual symbolic order doesn't simply exist on its own, but arises out of the deadlock of subjects who are opaque to themselves and to one another. In the standard 'idealist' view of the dialectic, the dialectical process moves continually upward to greater and greater transparency and reason – and in fact, in more radical forms of idealism, 'finite-temporal reality itself emerges *because* Reason, in its *inherent* movement, became involved in inconsistencies, and continues to exist only as long as Reason does not untangle them'.[3] That is, for the idealist view, material reality is the fallout from Reason's failure to become self-consistent. By contrast, the specifically *materialist* notion of the dialectic holds that even though the symbolic level is autonomous, an end-in-itself, it must nonetheless be grounded in the material level.[4] More than that, each level emerges out of contradiction and is itself marked by contradiction – the remainder of inert materiality is impossible to get rid of.

Thus far I have been using the example of the emergence of the big Other for the sake of convenience, because I have already discussed it at length in Chapter 2. In this context, however, it may seem to be question-begging – after all, the point here is to account for the place of human subjectivity, and the example of the big Other obviously presupposes the subject as a given. More than that, the reference to the irreducible remainder of materiality may lead one to believe that this is simply a fancy way of saying the same thing as 'vulgar' materialism: namely, that distinctively human phenomena are always chained to causal determinism. Žižek avoids this charge through two related moves in *The Indivisible Remainder*, both drawn from Schelling. First, he argues that the familiar level of causal determinism is *not* the bottom level of reality. The inert material remainder or 'brute fact' is therefore not the level of determinism – instead, 'the primordial, radically contingent fact, a fact which can in no way be accounted for, is freedom itself, a freedom bound by nothing, a freedom which, in a sense, *is* Nothing; and the problem is, rather, how this Nothing of the abyss of primordial freedom becomes entangled in the causal chains of Reason'.[5] The level of causal determinism must itself be accounted for, by demonstrating how it first arises out of the abyss of freedom or of pure potentiality. Second, he claims that it is precisely in *humanity* that the primordial freedom resurfaces within the realm of determinism, in the form of the self-relating void of subjectivity.

In the final section of *The Indivisible Remainder*, Žižek attempts to justify the two principles he draws from Schelling in terms of contemporary science. He equates the primordial abyss of freedom or pure potentiality with the realm of quantum physics, and he attempts to demonstrate indirectly that humanity is where this freedom reemerges from determinism by pointing out affinities between quantum phenomena and distinctively human phenomena. On the first point, the connection is relatively straightforward, in that quantum physics clearly operates in a way that seems baffling in light of conventional physics and our normal experience of reality:

> In classical physics, 'knowledge in the real' asserts its hold directly, without any delay – that is to say, things simply know what laws they are to obey – whereas quantum physics allows for a minimum of 'ontological cheating.'

Dialectical materialism, or the philosophy of freedom

A whole new domain is thus opened up, the domain of the shadowy pseudo-being of pure potentialities [. . .].[6]

The capacity for 'ontological cheating' depends on a gap between a particle's behaviour and other particles 'noticing' what it has done. Žižek draws a parallel between the rise of consistent and determined physical laws out of quantum interactions and the rise of the symbolic order among human subjects – thus our familiar physical reality amounts to a kind of 'big Other' among elementary particles. This parallel undoes the artificial distinction between humanity and nature, demonstrating that the aspects of human experience that are typically thought to be contradictory to what we know about nature actually arise from a more fundamental level of nature. The realm of physical law excludes potentiality, insofar as everything that is possible immediately happens, but 'in man [sic], possibility is no longer automatically realized but persists *qua* possibility – precisely as such, man stands for the point at which, in a kind of direct short circuit, the created universe regains the abyss of primordial Freedom'.[7] Resistance to the possibility that this affinity between humanity and the quantum realm exists testifies to the strength of the philosophical bias that wants to draw a sharp dividing line between humanity and nature.[8]

To put it in terms of his broader metaphysical scheme instead of his reading of Schelling, the goal of Žižek's use of quantum physics is to provide some scientific grounding for the idea that the realm of deterministic physical law is 'non-all'. This means not that there is some other positive order of being, but that there is a quasi-order of potentiality, of not-yet being, waiting to emerge:

> The emergence of human freedom can be accounted for only by the fact that nature itself is not a homogeneous 'hard' reality – that is to say, by the presence, beneath 'hard' reality, of another dimension of potentialities and fluctuations: it is as if, with human freedom, this uncanny universe of potentialities re-emerges and comes to light.[9]

This perspective on quantum physics as a necessary premise for human freedom can be considered one of Žižek's key metaphysical claims. In *The Indivisible Remainder*, however, there is a clear gap in Žižek's account. He shows how the big Other emerges out of the interaction of human subjects and how the quasi-'big Other' of physical law emerges out of the interaction of elementary particles, but he leaves out a crucial step – namely, how human subjectivity emerges out of the order of determinism. Žižek tackles that question in *The Parallax View* by means of an encounter with cognitive science, that is, the study of mental processes and their physical basis in the brain.

Self-consciousness as short circuit

The relationship between the brain and the mind is one of the key examples of the concept of parallax, which Žižek gets from Karatani and around which he organizes *The Parallax View*. The term parallax is used primarily in astronomy, and normally means 'the apparent displacement of an object (the shift of its position against a background), caused by a change in observational position that provides a new line of sight'.[10] Hence nearby stars will appear to be at a different place relative to the more distant 'background' stars when viewed from different locations on the earth's surface or at different points in the earth's rotation around the sun. Žižek's use of the concept is based on two shifts. First, he focuses on situations where a shift of perspective leads to more radical differences than a simple apparent change of location, that is, where a perspective change seems to produce a radical change in the object itself. For instance, light behaves as a particle under certain conditions and a wave under others, and it seems intuitively impossible that light could be both a particle and a wave at the same time. Second, Žižek argues – in a move that should be familiar at this point – that the parallax shift between the two incompatible views does not indicate only a gap in our knowledge, but an inherent conflict in the object itself. This can be thought of as removing the idea of a neutral 'background'. In the example of light, one might claim that there is no conflict between the particle and the wave, but that light is actually some third kind of thing whose nature we have not yet discovered, with this unknown state implicitly serving as the background against which the gap

Dialectical materialism, or the philosophy of freedom

between wave and particle is measured. For Žižek, however, light most fundamentally *is* the contradiction between particle and wave, meaning that it is *inherently* inconsistent before observation causes it to appear in one of its two incompatible modes. The concept of parallax thus serves as a way of uniting the concept of the Real as inherently conflictual and the dialectical shift from an epistemological obstacle to an ontological fault – and, in my reading at least, provides a way for Žižek to claim the key concepts in his work as more directly *his own*.[11]

In terms of the parallax gap between the brain and the mind, no one doubts that the brain is the seat of consciousness, yet it seems impossible to reconcile the brute materiality of the brain as a lump of organic material and our experience of consciousness. When faced with the findings of neurobiology and cognitive science – even the most basic, such as 'thought proceeds through the firing of neurons' or 'moods reflect the balance among certain chemicals in the brain' – one can hardly help feeling that one has been somehow 'deprived' of the intuitive experience of consciousness, that is, of *experience itself*. Žižek correlates this deprivation with the series of humiliations that humanity has suffered in the course of modern science, most notably Copernicus's displacement of humanity from the centre of the universe, Darwin's removal of the qualitative distinction between animal and human, and Freud's discovery of the unconscious. Renaissance humanism 'celebrated man as the crown of creation, the highest term in the chain of created beings, while modernity proper occurs only when man loses his privileged place and is reduced to just another element of reality – and correlative to this loss of privilege is the emergence of the subject as the pure immaterial void, not as a substantial part of reality'.[12]

This view of the emergence of modern subjectivity provides a kind of physical grounding for the view discussed in Chapter 2, where the void of subjectivity arises from the impossibility of substantially 'being' one's social role. Žižek also provides a *theological* grounding: Luther's view of humanity as 'divine shit' that 'fell out of God's anus'. As with his readings of Badiou and Schelling, Žižek does not immediately translate Luther's work into more neutral philosophical terms, but stays with the theological language, claiming that 'only within this Protestant logic of man's excremental identity can the true meaning of the Incarnation be formulated'. Whereas both Orthodoxy and Catholicism separate Christ from humanity – through idealizing him as an example to imitate or focusing on the 'symbolic exchange' involved in Christ's death for our sins, respectively –

> Protestantism, finally, posits the relationship as *real*, conceiving Christ as a God who, in his act of Incarnation, freely *identified himself with his own shit*, with the excremental Real that is man – and it is only at this level that the properly Christian notion of divine love can be apprehended, as love for the miserable excremental entity called 'man.'[13]

Thus the same movement that opened the door for the modern world, eventually destroying Christendom, provides the key to understanding what is most distinctive in Christianity[14] – an idea that makes sense in light of Žižek's contention that Christian love is a radically material love that aims at the part of the subject that escapes social inscription.

As discussed in the previous section, Christianity has most often reacted to the rise of modern science with a series of rearguard actions meant to somehow 'contain' science and keep it from undermining all religious belief. Although psychoanalysis is itself one of the results of the anti-humanist turn to modernity – and, Žižek argues, the most radical one[15] – it has developed its own equivalent to the 'God of the gaps' approach when it comes to the findings of cognitive science, using a variety of mutually contradictory argumentative strategies to try to maintain the prestige of psychoanalysis in the face of the progress of the brain sciences: 'First, cognitivism is factually wrong. Second, even if it is factually accurate, it is limited by its very scientific horizon. Third, cognitivism confirms what psychoanalysis predicted long ago about the functioning of the human mind . . .'[16] For Žižek, this approach is all wrong, even apart from the self-contradictions. In the broadest terms, with regard to the supposed dangers of scientific progress, Žižek argues that 'the temptation to be resisted is precisely the pseudo-ethical attitude of presenting scientific exploration as a temptation which can lead us into "going too far" – entering the forbidden territory (of biogenetic manipulations, and so on), and thus endangering the very core of our humanity'.[17] This stance

Dialectical materialism, or the philosophy of freedom

makes sense when one considers that, for Žižek, the progress of modern science led to the rise of the distinctively modern form of subjectivity as a self-relating void. More specifically, those who fear the progress of science due to its reductionism neglect the fact that 'contemporary sciences no longer aim at a simple and direct reduction of deceiving appearance to raw material reality: their central topic is, rather, that of the paradoxical pseudo-autonomy and efficiency of the "illusion", of illusory appearance, itself'.[18]

In essence, then, Žižek argues that contemporary science is already implicitly *practising* a non-reductive, dialectical form of materialism, but the philosophy of science has not caught up. In the specific case of the brain sciences, then, psychoanalysis – whose Lacanian form, at least, is for Žižek an integral part of dialectical materialism – should not be on the defensive against cognitive science, but should show how it can resolve cognitive science's deadlocks. Those deadlocks are indeed considerable – in Žižek's account, the student of cognitive science is stunned to discover 'how "everything goes," all possible answers coexist', with no clear consensus.[19] He divides the field into four basic positions, naming representative figures:

1. Radical/reductive materialism (Patricia and Paul Churchland): there simply are no qualia [mental phenomena], there is no 'consciousness,' these things exist only as a kind of 'naturalized' cognitive mistake. [...]
2. Antimaterialism (David Chalmers): consciousness-awareness cannot be accounted for in terms of other natural processes; it has to be conceived as a primordial dimension of nature, like gravity or magnetism.
3. The position of 'cognitive closure' which asserts the inherent unknowability of consciousness (Colin McGinn, even Steven Pinker): although consciousness emerged out of material reality, it is necessarily unknowable.
4. Nonreductive materialism (Daniel Dennett): consciousness exists, but it is the result of natural processes, and has a clear evolutionary function.[20]

For Žižek, the most convincing attempts to explain how consciousness arises out of the materiality of the brain get close to achieving a satisfying account, but nonetheless 'seem to miss its proper formulation', as though they were aiming at a 'missing concept'. Žižek argues that his dialectical materialism can supply this 'missing concept', namely: 'what German Idealism called self-relating negativity and Freud called "the death drive"'[21] – or, I might add, what Žižek (following Lacan) calls the 'feminine' mode of subjectivity.

Žižek's account of the rise of subjectivity out of the materiality of the brain is based primarily on the work of Antonio Damasio.[22] For Damasio, consciousness is most fundamentally 'the awareness of a *disturbance* of the organism's homeostasis caused by an encounter with an external (or internal) object [. . .]', an 'emotional reaction' to disruption.[23] The organism is able to detect this disturbance because of a series of mental maps that Damasio correlates with 'three kinds of Self'.[24] The lowest level is the Proto-Self, 'the neural "map" the organism forms of itself in order to be able to regulate and maintain its homeostasis'.[25] The Core Self is the organism's awareness of its surroundings, that is, its pre-verbal ability to provide a kind of account of the things that disturb its homeostasis. The final level is the Autobiographical Self, which is the organism's awareness of itself as continuous over time. The Autobiographical Self is completely dependent upon the Core Self, insofar as it 'is made of the virtual set of memories and projects which can be instantiated/actualized only in the living self-awareness of the Core Self'.[26] The Autobiographical Self is able to arise out of the Core Self because there are multiple levels of mental mapping. Initially, internal states and sense stimuli are directly captured in 'first-order maps'.[27] Attempts to account for the relationship between the organism and the object 'can be captured only in second-order neural maps', that is, mental maps that refer to the organism itself:

> This second-order mapping gives rise to a minimum of self-reflexivity: I not only know, I feel that I know (that it is I who know); I not only perceive an object, I am aware of myself perceiving it; I not only act, I feel that it is I who act. *I do not relate to (interact with) only an object: I relate to this relating 'as such.'* This is why consciousness is always also self-consciousness: [. . .] I am my knowledge of myself.[28]

Dialectical materialism, or the philosophy of freedom

Damasio claims that the Autobiographical Self is a separate entity from the Core Self, but Žižek argues that separating the two levels gets rid of the necessary element of reflexivity. Instead, the Autobiographical Self must be understood as arising out of a 'kind of short circuit between the two levels of representation', whereby the '*process of mapping* [. . .] *includes itself in the mapped process*'.[29] Such a short circuit produces a purely formal – that is, nonsubstantial – element of self-reflexivity, which for Žižek is the very definition of the subject.

From here, Žižek takes a further dialectical step. For Damasio, self-consciousness is emotional, the feeling of being conscious of oneself, but Žižek argues that this particular emotion changes the entire structure of the emotional realm. That is to say, whereas emotions originally served to allow the organism to maintain homeostasis, self-reflexivity allows for them to 'turn into goals-in-themselves' rather than being utilitarian signals: 'Here the role of pain is more elementary than that of pleasure: the elementary formula of the "autonomization" of pain and pleasure from their instrumental functions is that of *finding pleasure in pain itself*. Instead of reacting to pain in the normal survivalist way (avoiding it), I stick to it, deriving satisfaction from it.'[30] Thus, due to a purely formal element of reflexivity generated in an ever more complex attempt to maintain homeostasis, the organism is enabled to actively disturb its homeostasis. In the context of a discussion of Dennett, Žižek proposes 'the function of *blocking* as the elementary function of consciousness'. Consciousness, 'while in no way able to instigate a spontaneous act, can "freely" impede its actualization: it can veto it, say "No!" to a spontaneously emerging tendency'.[31] While consciousness is not able to disrupt the chain of deterministic causality directly, it can nevertheless block reactions to certain stimuli, opening up the space for a different and perhaps surprising act.

The anti-adaptive animal

In addition to situating the rise of subjectivity in its immediate biological context of the brain's neural mapping functions, Žižek also addresses the broader biological context of the evolutionary process. His guiding theme is 'the anti-Darwinian lesson of psychoanalysis repeatedly emphasized by Lacan: man's [*sic*] radical and fundamental *dis*-adaptation, *mal*-adaptation, to his environs'. I have already noted how the intervention of subjectivity allows a certain reversal whereby a system intended to maintain homeostasis enables the organism to wilfully disrupt its own homeostasis. This disconnect between emotions and their survivalist function is a privileged example of what Lacan calls the death drive, which 'consists in an "uncoupling" from immersion in one's environs, in following a certain automatism which ignores the demands of adaptation'. For Žižek, the death drive is what opens up the distinctively human realm of freedom: 'the "death drive" as a self-sabotaging structure represents the minimum of freedom, of a behaviour uncoupled from the utilitarian-survivalist attitude. The "death drive" means that the organism is no longer fully determined by its environs, that it "explodes/implodes" into a cycle of autonomous behavior'.[32]

Though it may seem initially counter-intuitive to claim that a 'drive' is the very principle of freedom, Žižek argues that such a conclusion is demanded by the very concept of freedom itself. Though quantum physics is important for Žižek, he agrees with Dennett in rejecting the common move that links freedom *directly* to the indeterminacy of the quantum level. Freedom is not simply a lack of determinism: 'as Kant knew, it means a specific mode of causality, the agent's self-determination'. Properly understood, then, true freedom, in the sense of self-determination, is a 'second-level reflexive causality: I am determined by causes (be it direct brute natural causes or motivations), and the space of freedom is not a magic gap in this first-level causal chain but my ability retroactively to choose/determine which causes will determine me'.[33] I can only act *within* the realm of physical causality, but freedom means that I am not directly determined by an outside causality insofar as I am responsible for paradoxically choosing the very causes of my actions.

The space for this self-determination only opens up through the death drive as a purely negative gesture of refusal. This gesture arises out of the fact that the subject is 'originally passive: [. . .] what I am originally "aware of" is that I am not in control, that my design has misfired, that things are just drifting by'.[34] Once this initial refusal takes place, the relationship of the human subject to its surroundings is fundamentally changed. Žižek's key illustration

Dialectical materialism, or the philosophy of freedom

of this principle is the difference between human and animal sexuality. Drawing on the work of evolutionary psychologist Geoffrey Miller,[35] Žižek argues that human intelligence is one of many secondary features intended to help draw a mate, which Miller calls 'fitness indicators'. These features occur in many species, and though they are, from a purely utilitarian standpoint, a waste of the animal's energy, they are nonetheless impressive to potential partners, since they indicate that the animal has strength to spare. Here Žižek uses an example from human behaviour: 'if a girl gets a big diamond ring from her lover, this is not just a signal of his wealth but, simultaneously, a proof of it – he has to be rich in order to be able to afford it . . . .'.[36]

The specifically human element arises when 'what originally served as an instrument or indicator [is] elevated into an end in itself'.[37] Language, for instance, has now clearly exceeded its initial role as a means of impressing a mate. But this disconnect between the original purpose goes beyond secondary traits meant to impress others to the indicators meant as signals for the organism (pleasure and pain). The best example is human sexuality, which is disconnected from the original goal of reproduction and 'becomes an aim in itself, so that the human animal spends large amounts of time pursuing this aim, planning it in all its details, even directly blocking the original goal (through contraception)'.[38] Sexuality in this sense then spills over into all areas of life, as in the well-known possibility of turning virtually any utterance into a sexual innuendo. This metaphorical 'sexualization' of all human activities is so thoroughgoing that it even applies to its original metaphorical ground:

> The specific quality of human sexuality has nothing to do with the immediate, rather stupid reality of copulation, including preparatory mating rituals; only when animal coupling gets caught in the self-referential vicious circle of drive, in the protracted repetition of its failure to reach the impossible Thing [i.e., *jouissance*], do we get what we call sexuality, that is, sexual activity itself gets sexualized.[39]

Thus Žižek claims that 'the Catholic attitude of allowing sex only for the goal of procreation' misses the specifically human element in sexuality and thereby 'debases it to animal coupling'.[40] Here one could draw a connection with Žižek's critique of the 'perverse core of Christianity', discussed in the previous chapter. The 'natural law' on which Catholic teaching on sexuality purports to be based is a particularly interesting case of an 'attempt to install the law artificially, *in the desperate hope that we will then take this self-posited limitation "seriously"* [. . .]'.[41]

The 'sexualization' of human activity, turning means into ends in themselves, has its correlate in the reduction of 'biological survival itself [. . .] to a mere means'[42] – that is, a complete inversion of natural selection. For instance, the truly human approach to eating is not to eat sheerly for survival, but to continue living so that (among other things) we can enjoy the pleasure of eating. This inversion is one of the key examples of what it means for dialectical materialism to be non-reductive: human culture is not simply a continuation of natural selection, a kind of super-adaptivity, but is rather an end-in-itself.[43] The dialectical nature of this process is what allows 'higher' activities such as culture to arise out of the 'lower' survival strategies and what grants those 'higher' activities their own autonomy. Nevertheless, the materialist element means that the original grounding is never left behind: even if I choose to survive only in order to eat, I still must *survive* in order to eat. To put it differently: the 'higher' process does not have to *serve* the 'lower' – that is the position of 'vulgar' or reductive materialism – yet the 'higher' process can never escape its grounding in the 'lower', as a radical idealism might claim.[44]

Moreover, Žižek's dialectical materialism will not allow humanity to be conceived as some kind of isolated aberration that disrupts a previously harmonious nature – the conflictuality goes 'all the way down'. Drawing on quantum physics, Žižek claims that the universe originated in some disruption that interrupted the harmonious balance of the abyss of pure potentiality, which is to say that existence itself emerged out of a fundamental imbalance. With this in mind, Žižek draws a more radical connection between humanity and the quantum realm: 'the features we refer to in order to emphasize man's unique status – the constitutive imbalance, the "out-of-joint[ness]", on account of which man is an "unnatural" creature, "nature sick unto death" – must somehow already be at work in nature itself'.[45] To understand

Dialectical materialism, or the philosophy of freedom

humanity properly, then, one must not follow the typical procedure of reducing all human behaviour to some 'natural' explanation. Instead, one must throw out the customary idea of nature as internally consistent and harmonious.

Having come full-circle in terms of Žižek's engagement with science, it may be helpful to pause here and consider an example from twentieth-century theology that closely parallels Žižek's approach, namely, Wolfhart Pannenberg's *Anthropology in Theological Perspective*.[46] In this massively erudite and ambitious work, Pannenberg relates the traditional themes of theological anthropology to the full range of sciences that take the human being as their object, including biology (represented by behaviourism), psychoanalysis, social theory and history, among many others. This investigation is founded in the conviction that Christian theology, if it is to be taken seriously, must defend its universal anthropological claims *within* the field of the human sciences.[47] He distinguishes himself from the traditional 'God of the gaps' approach in two ways. First, he rejects the idea that theologians can use the findings of the human sciences as a kind of neutral tool, because their secular nature means that they are intrinsically biased against theology.[48] Rather than using that as a reason to utterly reject the findings of human science and retreat into a mere assertion of revelation, he argues that the secular account must be expanded so that its repressed theological element can come to the surface. Specifically, he argues that the key categories of traditional theological anthropology, sin and the image of God, can shed further light on the 'secular' data.[49] The basic conviction here is that if theology is *true*, then it must also be *necessary* – and therefore one must take a step beyond merely attempting to show how theology and the human sciences agree to actively intervening into the human sciences to help resolve their problems and contradictions.

The parallel here is clear: both Pannenberg and Žižek use the same basic method of getting beyond the 'God of the gaps' approach (or its psychoanalytic equivalent). Interestingly, however, though Pannenberg's stance may initially sound more dogmatic than Žižek's, in practice Pannenberg is much more willing to let the sciences 'push back' on his theological work. That is to say, Pannenberg admits that many traditional theological claims cannot be responsibly advanced in light of contemporary scientific findings – most notably the idea that humanity started off in a perfect state in the Garden of Eden – and so one must dispense with them.⁵⁰ Pannenberg even rejects many modern attempts to extract some 'deeper meaning' from the story, because they logically presuppose an original state that cannot possibly have existed. One explanation for this difference, however, might be the simple fact that psychoanalysis arose entirely within the modern period, after the advent of science. Yet psychoanalysis does bring certain 'baggage' with it, and one might wonder, for example, how Žižek's reading of Judaism may have turned out differently if he had allowed himself simply to admit that Freud's account of the origin of the Jewish people is almost certainly not historically accurate, or more generally how his understanding of the rise of Christianity might have been enriched by more attention to historical scholarship. There does, however, still appear to be time for more historical research, given the continued importance of Christianity in *The Parallax View*, to which I now turn.

Theological materialism

Žižek's position on Christianity in *The Parallax View* is essentially the position at which he arrived in *The Puppet and the Dwarf*. The most significant new engagement with theology is an extended critical reading of Kierkegaard, which makes up the bulk of *The Parallax View*'s second chapter, entitled 'Building-Blocks for a Materialist Theology'. More striking than any change in content, however, is where he puts the bulk of his reflections on Christianity – namely, in the first major division of *The Parallax View*, devoted to the concept of 'ontological difference', which Žižek calls 'the ultimate parallax which conditions our very access to reality'.⁵¹ Ontological difference is a key concept from the work of Martin Heidegger, the philosopher who has arguably had the greatest influence on theology in the twentieth century and an increasingly important figure in Žižek's work from *The Ticklish Subject* forward.⁵² With the term ontological difference, Heidegger names the distinction between 'beings', in the sense of particular entities, and 'Being' itself, and he argues that philosophy, nearly from the moment of its inception, has forgotten about

Dialectical materialism, or the philosophy of freedom

Being, contenting itself with beings. Thus Heidegger undertakes to reopen the question of the meaning of Being, over the course of a voluminous and complex body of work.

Many interpretations of the concept of ontological difference have been proposed. Some scholars, for instance, believe that ontological difference names the difference between particular beings' bare existence and their essence, or 'between the All of reality and something else which, with regard to reality, cannot but appear as "Nothing"'. Žižek rejects both these views.[53] In their place, he proposes – perhaps unsurprisingly – a reading of ontological difference based on Lacan's formulae of sexuation. Traditional metaphysics grounds the order of being in an infinite supreme being that is, strictly speaking, 'beyond being', and so this position falls under the 'masculine' logic of the constitutive exception. By contrast, 'the ontological difference proper is feminine: reality is non-all, but there is nothing beyond-outside it, and this Nothing is Being itself'.[54] Ontological difference means that the domain of beings is finite, but also non-totalizable – where the classical supreme being has power over the All, the Heideggerian notion of Being denotes a gap that renders the realm of beings inherently incomplete.

Thus far, the basic concepts at work should be familiar from this and previous chapters. Yet in dealing with this most fundamental parallax gap, Žižek also reveals what is ultimately at stake in his ontology: ethics. Since I have so far in this chapter focused mainly on his discussion of science, some readers may think that Žižek conceives dialectical materialism as simply a 'better' philosophy of science, offering a more adequate account of specifically human phenomena. Even within the strictly scientific domain, however, it is clear that more is at stake, as when he lays down a clear alternative: 'either subjectivity is an illusion, or reality is *in itself* (and not only epistemologically) not-All'.[55] One might fairly ask: why *not* say that subjectivity is an illusion? What would be lost? Within Žižek's scheme, where every theory of subjectivity implies an ethics,[56] one would lose a lot, perhaps everything. If subjectivity were an illusion, then our ethical struggles would be meaningless play-acting, would fail to 'count'. Žižek's basic concern here is one that echoes through the history of Christian theology: the principle that moral judgement is impossible apart from free will, a principle to which even the most radical predestinarians have tried to do justice. The key question in Žižek's context is '*within what ontology is the ethical dimension proper possible* without being reduced to an epiphenomenon [. . .]?'[57] That is, within what ontology are we ethically 'playing for keeps'? Žižek begins by rejecting two commonly held views: on the one hand, the idea that our ethical experience is ultimately just an illusion that would be dispelled if we had full knowledge of the causes of our actions, and on the other hand, the idea that ethics must be grounded in some transcendent beyond. Though apparently diametrically opposed, both views share a separation or incompatibility between being and the ethical dimension. In their place, Žižek proposes a dialectical materialist scheme wherein the ethical emerges from the gaps and inconsistencies at the heart of the order of being itself.

The second half of Žižek's discussion of ontological difference, then, consists in laying out the specific form of ethics demanded by dialectical materialism, in large part through a critical reading of Kierkegaard. His primary interest in Kierkegaard is the 'logic of meaningless sacrifice ([Kierkegaard's] term for it is "infinite resignation")', which for Žižek means that 'only a thin, almost imperceptible line separates Kierkegaard from dialectical materialism proper'.[58] Kierkegaard's famous exposition of the stance of the 'knight of infinite resignation' is found in *Fear and Trembling*. There his task is to attempt to understand Abraham's sacrifice of Isaac, which he breaks down into two moments: first, Abraham must completely give up Isaac for dead even before beginning the journey to Mount Moriah and must correlatively give up any attempt to make his decision to sacrifice Isaac intelligible to anyone; second, Abraham must somehow turn around and receive Isaac back gladly, without missing a beat. Johannes de Silentio, Kierkegaard's pseudonymous 'author', understands the first moment as 'infinite resignation', a kind of radical Stoicism verging on despair, where the subject renounces or sacrifices everything that has supplied his life with meaning. What Silentio can never understand, however, is Abraham's ability to shift instantly from that stance to joyfully getting Isaac back – such a move is available only to the 'knight of faith', and Silentio remains within the ethical dimension, unable to make the 'leap of faith' into the religious.

Though Kierkegaard makes much of the difference between the 'aesthetic' or purely pleasure-seeking life and the properly 'ethical' life of duty, Žižek argues that the true parallax in Kierkegaard's thought is between both of those stages and the third, 'religious' stage. The aesthetic and ethical stances fail not because of 'their respective positive characteristics, but [because of] their very formal nature: the fact that, in both cases, the subject wants to live a consistent mode of existence' – that is, either to seek pleasure at all costs or to do one's duty at all costs – 'and thus disavows the radical antagonism of the human situation'. The properly religious stance embraces this underlying conflictuality, the fact that 'there is no guarantee that Abraham's decision to kill Isaac is not his private madness'.[59] Where Kierkegaard goes wrong for Žižek is in reducing the 'religious' stage to another positive stage, guaranteed by God, and here Žižek draws an explicit parallel between Kierkegaard and the Lacanian reading of Descartes. As indicated in Chapter 2, Descartes' radical doubt exposes the subject to be a pure empty void, but he pulls back from this void by anchoring himself in the famous *cogito ergo sum*, 'I think therefore I am', from which he arrives at the idea of a trustworthy God who guarantees the accuracy of the subject's knowledge. In the same way, Kierkegaard's 'infinite resignation' opens up the abyss of meaninglessness or absurdity: 'What Kierkegaardian "infinite resignation" confronts us with is pure Meaning, Meaning as such, reduced to the empty form of Meaning which remains after I have renounced all humanly determined finite Meaning: pure, unconditional Meaning can appear (and it *has* to appear) only as nonsense.'[60] Like Descartes, however, Kierkegaard backs away from this abyss by grounding himself in a God who can guarantee the meaningfulness of his life.[61] For this reason, Žižek argues that 'Kierkegaard's procedure remains transcendental: his question is that of the *conditions of possibility* of leading a meaningful life, and belief emerges as the only truly viable answer'.[62]

The shift from the 'transcendental' Kierkegaard to the 'materialist' Kierkegaard consists in removing any positive God – a move that is perhaps faithful to certain strands of Kierkegaard's thought:

> Kierkegaard's God is strictly correlative to the ontological openness of reality, to our relating to reality as unfinished, 'in becoming.' 'God' is the name for the Absolute Other against which we can measure the thorough contingency of

reality – as such, it cannot be conceived as any kind of Substance, as the Supreme Thing (that would again make him part of Reality, its true Ground).[63]

In ethical terms, this brings Kierkegaard in line with the only possible modern stance, according to which '"God" is ultimately the name for the purely negative gesture of meaningless sacrifice'.[64] Thus, in place of the logic whereby the 'knight of infinite resignation' is finally repaid for his sacrifice by being able to reinstall some particular meaning for his life, Žižek proposes that one should carry through 'infinite resignation' to its logical extreme: after giving up all determinate meaning, one should sacrifice the very idea of meaning itself, sacrifice the very notion of any outside guarantee. The completely 'meaningless' sacrifice escapes the logic of sacrifice, not in the classically Christian mode where Christ's sacrifice pays up all outstanding debts, but by virtue of being a pure and absolute loss – a sacrifice that renders the very notion of 'sacrifice' nonsensical. Normal neurotic subjects tend to feel guilty if they receive any benefit from doing their ethical duty, since they instinctively understand ethics in terms of sacrifice, whereas Žižek is proposing a radical ethics that renounces even the very notion of sacrifice, allowing the subject to receive benefit from their ethical choices without guilt.[65] To put it in terms of the Abraham story, then, the 'sacrifice of sacrifice' is what opens up the space for receiving Isaac back joyfully rather than being disappointed that one's stance of heroic resignation has been somehow tainted.

The name for this ethical choice of the worst – for which the psychoanalytic cure provides the ultimate model – is the death drive, which for Žižek represents most fundamentally what it means to be human and what it means to be radically free. Žižek relates the death drive to Kantian ethics, where the moral law is a completely empty command to do duty for duty's sake. This empty commandment is not imposed from the outside, but rather stands for every subject's duty to be self-legislating and to take full responsibility for that self-legislation – even the fact that something is our 'duty cannot serve as an excuse for doing our duty'.[66] Thus unconditional obedience to duty does not mean, as some have argued, that one must simply obey society's laws:

Dialectical materialism, or the philosophy of freedom

Kant's true aim, rather, is to point out how *the very need of an external master is a deceptive lure*: man needs a master in order to conceal from himself the deadlock of his own difficult freedom and self-responsibility. In this precise sense, a truly enlightened 'mature' human being is a subject who *no longer needs a master*, who can fully assume the heavy burden of defining his own limitations.[67]

In his discussion of cognitive science, Žižek equates the level of drive with the possibility of the human organism being truly self-determining in the sense of choosing its own causes, and here he ties it to the Kantian ideal of the ethical subject as self-legislating. Perhaps paradoxically, however, Žižek also ties the level of drive to 'the "theological" dimension without which, for Benjamin, revolution cannot win',[68] echoing the passage from *Sublime Object* discussed in Chapter 3. Thus just as Kierkegaard's God must be understood as the lack of an overarching guarantee of life's meaningfulness, so also the properly 'theological' level is that which exposes the human subject as self-legislating, with no master – meaning that for Žižek, 'theology', properly understood, refers to the most radical atheism.

The politics of refusal, or waiting on the Holy Spirit

As the reference to the role of theology in 'revolution' indicates, the end goal remains political, and so the question is: what politics corresponds to dialectical materialism? Though Žižek devotes the final third of *The Parallax View* – along with the entire second 'interlude' (on anti-Semitism) and several lengthy passages scattered throughout – to the question of the political, the only 'positive' political programme he espouses is an entirely negative one. Inspired by the enigmatic title character of Herman Melville's short story 'Bartleby the Scrivener', who answers every request with an 'I would prefer not to', Žižek concludes *The Parallax View* with a politics of thoroughgoing refusal:

> We can imagine the varieties of such a gesture [of refusal] in today's public space: not only the obvious 'There are great

chances of a new career here! Join us!' – 'I would prefer not to'; but also 'Discover the depths of your true self, find inner peace!' – 'I would prefer not to'; or 'Are you aware of how our environment is endangered? Do something for ecology!' – 'I would prefer not to'; or 'What about all the racial and sexual injustices that we witness all around us? Isn't it time to do more?' – 'I would prefer not to.'[69]

Once again, Žižek invokes the concept of the parallax gap, arguing that 'the very frantic and engaged activity of constructing a new order is sustained by an underlying "I would prefer not to" which forever reverberates in it . . . The difficulty of imagining the New is the difficulty of imagining Bartleby in power.'[70]

Yet here, as always, the emphasis is on the negative move as the absolutely necessary first step, and in imagining what a radically 'Bartlebean' position might look like, he argues that one must renounce

> all the forms of resisting which help the system to reproduce itself by ensuring our participation in it – today 'I would prefer not to' is not primarily 'I would prefer not to participate in the market economy, in capitalist competition and profiteering,' but – much more problematically for some – 'I would prefer not to give to charity to support a Black orphan in Africa, engage in the struggle to prevent oil-drilling in a wildlife swamp, send books to educate our liberal-feminist-spirited women in Afghanistan . . .'[71]

That is to say, radically refusing the system includes refusing the devices whereby we distance ourselves from it, convincing ourselves that we are not 'part of the problem'. In the context of Žižek's entire trajectory, which I have mapped out over the course of these four chapters, this final position is a classic example of the dialectical 'negation of negation': at the end of his 'early' stage (Chapter 1), he renounced liberalism; in his 'middle' stage (Chapters 2 and 3), he 'retreated into theory' in order to find a new political option and for a time seemed to be advocating simply switching masters for its own sake; and finally in his 'present' stage, he advances this very renunciation itself as his political option. As he says in *The Ticklish Subject*, '"Negation of negation" is thus nothing but repetition at its purest: in the first move, a certain gesture is accomplished and fails; then, in the second move, this same gesture is simply *repeated*.'[72]

For Žižek, the Bartleby stance represents the greatest possible revolutionary violence, a far greater level of disruptive force than any violence in the literal sense: 'There is no violent *quality* in it; the violence pertains to its very immobile, inert, insistent, impassive *being*.'[73] Whatever its value politically, such a stance certainly does have a jarring effect – I can think of no better response to Žižek's position than the words of some of Christ's bewildered listeners: 'This teaching is difficult; who can accept it?'[74] To attempt to convince anyone to accept this teaching is ultimately Žižek's own responsibility, one that he will doubtless undertake in many voluminous works over the many years of productivity that he still has before him. A large part of such an effort will have to do with specifying what Bartleby's revolution might look like, how we will be able to recognize it if and when it arises.[75] As a way of concluding my exposition of Žižek's work, then, I would like to take the risk of exceeding my mandate as an 'introducer' in order to suggest a direction that Žižek's development of this politics of refusal might take. One way to go about this would of course be to insist that if Žižek knew what was good for him, he would look into something that is important to me – for example, that he should take biblical scholarship more seriously, or that he should complicate his use of gendered language and pay more attention to feminism and queer theory, or that he should sit down and work his way through Barth's *Church Dogmatics*, or that he should engage with Latin American liberation theology. Doubtless Žižek would respond to such suggestions with a rousing 'I would prefer not to!'

Thus instead of abstractly asserting my own opinion over against Žižek or attempting to graft some particular content into his work, I will attempt to work with the materials already at hand, making connections that Žižek seems not yet to have made, at least not explicitly – that is to say, I am attempting to construct this position from *within* his work as I understand it. The first thing to note is that in *The Parallax View*, Žižek maintains the parallel between Lacan's idea of a collective of analysts and 'the Holy Spirit', which serves as the model of a sociality without a master signifier, that is, a non-ideological order. Given that his work on

Christianity aimed to give an account of how the new social form he calls 'the Holy Spirit' arose through an event (the death of Christ) that opened up the 'unplugged' diaspora stance of Judaism to all nations, one might expect Žižek to search for *specific* ways to 'repeat' that Pauline sequence in the contemporary context.

There are some signs in *The Parallax View* that he is moving in that direction. On the one hand, he sharpens his analysis of the contemporary situation as a culture of hedonism that is undermining the 'classical' forms of subjectivity outlined by traditional psychoanalysis. He refuses, however, the notion that psychoanalysts must work for the reimposition of traditional paternal authority in order to stave off the breakdown of normative Oedipal forms of subjectivity – to do so would be to give in to the temptation of perversion, the very temptation that, for Žižek, Paul is striving to avoid in Romans 7. Just as Žižek's Paul institutes a daring perspective shift that transforms the greatest defeat (Christ's death) into the greatest triumph (the resurrection conceived as the new social link called 'Holy Spirit'), Žižek proposes that 'it is only today that we encounter in our daily lives the basic libidinal deadlock around which psychoanalysis circulates'[76] – that is, the cultural shifts that seem to be undermining psychoanalysis actually represent an unprecedented opportunity. On the other hand, Žižek maintains the idea that the goal is to arrive at the Jewish 'unplugged' stance toward the law. Against the French psychoanalyst Jean-Claude Milner, who argues that one must oppose 'Judaism' (by which he means the attachment to family and tradition), Žižek argues that one must get out of the constant European mindset of anti-Semitism, for which the 'Jew' stands for 'the obstacle to a unified Europe'. Instead, Žižek proposes that one should 'fight for a non-All Europe as a truly new political form' which 'will no longer need the "Jew" as its limit-obstacle, as its constitutive exception'. The logic of anti-Semitism, which for Žižek is the very model of ideology (see Chapter 1), always leads at least part of the way down the road to a 'final solution' that would get rid of the Jews once and for all – to combat this horrifying logic, Žižek proposes that 'the "solution to the Jewish problem"' is 'that we all turn into "Jews," into *objets petit a*, into exceptions'.[77]

A 'non-all' political form in which everyone is an *objet petit a* – this could stand as a brief formula for a political form modelled on Lacan's

Dialectical materialism, or the philosophy of freedom

'discourse of the analyst' or the 'Holy Spirit'. The question is how to get there. It seems clear that the route of putting literally everyone through psychoanalytic treatment is unworkable. On the other hand, Žižek argues that the distinctively Jewish stance of being 'unplugged' from the national substance is being undermined from within by Zionism, which threatens to turn the Jews into simply one nation among others.[78] A potential way out of this dilemma is to detach the 'Jewish' stance from the Jews as a particular group, isolating its formal structure and seeing if there are other groups where it might be present. Drawing a parallel that some will likely find offensive for a variety of reasons, Žižek claims that it is actually Muslims who today are the object of 'anti-Semitic' logic – in Israel, in Europe and in the global 'War on Terror', Muslims are cast as the ultimate obstacle. This parallel seems to me to be a blind alley, however. If the distinctively 'Jewish' character of the Jewish community is threatened by the existence of Israel as a nation-state, wouldn't that be even more true of Islam, given that explicitly Islamic political movements already hold power in several countries?

To find a more productive parallel, in my view, one must note what is important about Judaism in Žižek's work on Christianity: namely, that it represents a social body whose members are, for whatever reason, 'automatically' inducted into the 'unplugged' stance toward the law. Only on such a ground can the 'Holy Spirit' possibly arise as a mass phenomenon. Drawing on Badiou's general notion that a truth-event arises among those excluded from a given situation, Žižek initially proposes the unemployed and the Palestinians as possible sites for an event,[79] but his ultimate example is the explosion of urban slums in the Third World – lawless zones made up of improvised housing with minimal social structuring. On a formal level, Žižek draws certain parallels between the Marxist concept of the proletariat and the slum dwellers, but he ultimately breaks with the Marxist tradition in privileging a group whose political situation, rather than economic exploitation, marks them as a possible site for an event. Whereas the vast populations of refugees still maintain some minimal, if negative, link to a legal order, 'a slum-dweller is the one with regard to whom the Power renounces its right to exert full control and discipline, finding it more appropriate to let him dwell in the twilight zone of slums'.[80] In this sense, one might say that the slum dweller, like Job, is confronted with the impotence of the big Other – the capitalist economic system and its corresponding political structures simply have nothing to offer the slum dweller.

The slums, then, carry the potential for a social grouping that would be genuinely 'unplugged' from the capitalist system. At this time, Žižek sees this potential as being in its very early stages, but nevertheless has a certain guarded optimism: 'What we should be looking for are the signs of the new forms of social awareness that will emerge from the slum collectives: they will be the seeds of the future.'[81] To make explicit the connection with the rise of Christianity, then, one must look for some type of event to emerge out of the slums that will somehow allow the 'Gentiles' who are plugged into capitalism to 'unplug' and join in the creation of something new. And what does one do while waiting for such an event? Žižek's own practice may provide some clues: practising ideology critique as a form of hysterical provocation, returning to the 'missed opportunities' of the revolutionary past with a view toward what it might mean to redeem them, and trying to trace out the theoretical shape of the event and of what it might look like to 'unplug' – in short, to wait in hope, so as to be ready to greet the event when it comes. But if the Christ-event is any indication, one must expect the event to come not 'in glory', but in humility and shame, as foolishness, as a stumbling block, as a scandal. Nevertheless, it remains unclear to me, based on Žižek's writings, what one can expect the collective bound together by the 'Holy Spirit' to look like in practice, beyond very abstract formal characteristics. This very lack of clarity, however, may well reflect the intrinsic difficulty of imagining a genuine break at the present historical moment.

Having made my way through Žižek's intellectual trajectory from *Sublime Object* to his most recent major work, *The Parallax View*, and offered a possible indication of where his trajectory may lead him, I have only a few tasks to achieve before bringing this book to a close. In the next and final chapter, I will first provide an overview of the theological themes discussed thus far and address the arguments of theologians who have written on Žižek to date. I will then conclude by offering some suggestions for future theological research, both in terms of Žižek's theological work and certain aspects of his thought that are not immediately theological but might nonetheless provide resources for theologians.

Chapter 5

Theological responses

The first four chapters were, broadly speaking, written from a position 'internal' to Žižek's work. In them, I gave an account of Žižek's work since *Sublime Object*, and my focus was naturally on his work in theology, in two respects. First, I devoted most of my attention to the areas of his thought most directly connected with his work on Christianity. Second, I attempted to develop a narrative of his overall trajectory that would make sense of his turn to theology. Though demonstrating it is perhaps beyond the scope of an introductory work, I would argue that an approach centred on his use of theology – that is, an approach that views his turn to theology as a *necessary* move within his project rather than a transitory response to an academic fad – is an intrinsically good way to get at what Žižek is doing and to track the development of his position.[1]

This chapter takes up a different, more 'external' stance toward Žižek's work. Instead of attempting to account for the place of theology in Žižek's project, I will look at the relationship of theology to Žižek. After briefly taking inventory of the theological themes that Žižek addresses, I will give an overview of the responses of various theologians to Žižek's work. To date, there have been relatively few such responses, but those that have appeared come from a variety of perspectives. Some of the most extended responses come from the Radical Orthodoxy school, with whom Žižek collaborated on the recent edited volume *Theology and the Political: The New Debate*,[2] but perhaps the most important in terms of actually using Žižek as a source for theological reflection can be found in Clayton Crockett's recent book *Interstices of the Sublime: Theology and Psychoanalytic Theory*.[3] In addition to Crockett and the members of the Radical Orthodoxy school who have responded in most detail to Žižek, I will address several other perspectives – both in terms of outlining responses that have appeared and interpreting the silence from certain quarters as a kind of response in itself.

From there, I will turn to possible avenues for future research, which will allow me to discuss some areas of Žižek's thought that did not fit into my scheme in the first four chapters – most notably the aspect of his work for which he is arguably most famous: his pervasive use of popular culture. Following up on my comparison between Žižek and Pannenberg's approach to the sciences, I will bring Žižek's analysis of popular culture into relation with Paul Tillich's 'method of correlation', as laid out in the first volume of his *Systematic Theology*.[4] I will then put forward Žižek's work on the revolutionary tradition as a model for being faithful to a tradition under radically changed circumstances. Both of these sections reflect my general belief that theologians are too prone to focus exclusively on philosophical texts that deal overtly with religion or theology and in so doing often skip over other areas that can be just as relevant to theological reflection. Finally, I will bring this chapter to a close by turning again to Žižek's work on Christianity, reading it as an echo of two of the greatest challenges to arise within Christian theology in the twentieth century: Dietrich Bonhoeffer's notion of a 'religionless Christianity' and Thomas J. J. Altizer's theology of the 'death of God'.

An inventory of theological themes

Before turning to the responses that have appeared to date and my suggestions for further responses, it seems appropriate to review precisely what is being responded to. As the first four chapters, and particularly the third and fourth, have indicated, there is much in Žižek's work that is of direct interest to theologians. He stakes out positions on many traditional theological loci, on questions of ethics, on issues of biblical interpretation and church history, and on the meaning of theological language in general. In addition, he responds to the work of several figures in the history of Christian theology.

Žižek develops his own theory of the incarnation, where in place of a 'substance', the divine element in Christ is a certain gap or lack separating him from other humans and the human element in God is also a gap inherent to God. Just as in the early church, then, Žižek's account of the incarnation is necessarily tied to the doctrine of the Trinity, that is, an account of what the incarnation tells us about God's 'internal' life. Žižek's approach here is Hegelian rather than orthodox: God (the Father) fully empties himself into Christ, and Christ in turn is resurrected as the Holy Spirit, conceived as the unique bond uniting the early Christian collectives. In a sense, Žižek can also be said to have a 'theological anthropology', insofar as Christ embodies what it means to be truly human – the fundamental level of humanity being understood in terms of the Lacanian 'excremental remainder' or *objet petit a*. If not for the fact that his theological positions are paradoxically grounded in a radical atheism, one might even be tempted to develop a systematic theology along Žižekian lines.

In terms of ethics, Žižek shares with the mainstream of the Christian theological tradition an insistence on the link between the reality of human freedom and the possibility of a meaningful ethical life. He also places great stress on the specifically Christian concept of love, which he interprets along materialist lines. His analysis of the figure of Job simultaneously as the representative of the distinctively Jewish stance and as the first critic of ideology implicitly brings his entire theory of ideology critique into the realm of theological reflection, in line with contemporary theologians from a variety of liberation traditions who have underlined the subversive qualities of the Jewish prophetic tradition. In addition, his continual critique of anti-Semitism as the archetype of ideology in the modern world, along with his claim that Christian anti-Semitism reflects Christianity's loss of its inmost core, is in line with the general postwar trend of repentance for anti-Semitism and dialogue with Judaism in Christian theological and ecclesiastical circles alike. On the other hand, Žižek's polemic against Buddhism is out of line with the general trend toward interreligious dialogue.

The central question of biblical and historical interpretation for Žižek's work is the relationship between Judaism and Christianity, and his final position, presented in *The Puppet and the Dwarf*, is difficult to place in traditional terms. His position is supercessionist insofar as Žižek clearly believes that the movement inaugurated by Paul was 'better' than Judaism – and the mark of this superiority is, in general terms, the same distinction between ethnic particularity and universality that has so often figured in supercessionist accounts. Yet his brand of supercessionism is a peculiar one. On the one hand, in contrast with most theologians in the tradition, Žižek views the particularly Jewish stance toward the law as the *solution* rather than the problem and argues that Paul's preaching of the death of Christ opens up the Jewish stance to Gentiles. As a result, Christianity must maintain its reference to Judaism or else lose its most distinctive traits. On the other hand, the key betrayal of 'actual existing Christianity' is its rejection of the Jewish stance toward the law, meaning that it has relapsed into paganism. Accordingly, Judaism is 'better' than post-Pauline Christianity.[5] If supercessionism in the classic sense means that Christianity is a separate religion over against Judaism, then Žižek is arguing against a supercessionist position – Paul's movement must be understood as a movement *within* Judaism – yet the assertion of the Pauline position as the end goal is doubtless one that few Jews would embrace.[6] In addition to the relationships among Judaism, Paul's collectives, and the actual existing church, Žižek analyses, much more briefly and elliptically, the relationship among the three great strands of the Christian tradition: Orthodoxy, Christianity and Protestantism. Here he has a clear preference for Protestantism, implicitly endorsing the Protestant claim to represent a return to the core of the gospel – but he understands the core of the gospel to be very different from the teachings of traditional Protestantism, arguing that the return to the authentic gospel and the turn to secular modernity go hand in hand.

    Žižek's view of theological language has two related prongs: the need for 'mythological' language and the true meaning of properly 'theological' language.[7] As demonstrated first of all by his reading of Schelling and then in several other places already indicated in previous chapters, Žižek claims that one must resist the temptation to remove the 'mythological' elements from a text in order to distil its true meaning from what remains. In terms of biblical scholarship, this means that Žižek would be opposed to a 'demythologizing' approach to scriptural interpretation: he insists that the true meaning of a text can only be found in and through the mythological language. Even though he shows only as much interest in the life of Christ as Paul does, it seems fair to conclude that Žižek would object to something like Thomas Jefferson's edited Bible, which removes miracles and other supernatural references in order to get at Christ's pure moral teaching. Nevertheless, Žižek does not accept the traditional notion that theological language serves first of all to give an account of supernatural entities and events. Instead, following Benjamin, he defines 'theology' in terms of redemption, meaning a reactivation of the past. On the political level, this reactivation is found in the attempt to redeem previous failed attempts at revolution, and on the personal level, it is found in the 'reboot' of the fundamental fantasy brought about through the psychoanalytic cure.

Throughout his career, and in particular in the period since *The Ticklish Subject*, certain theologians have played an important role in Žižek's work. His two most important theological points of reference are St Paul and Kierkegaard, but he also devotes considerable attention to Pascal, G. K. Chesterton, C. S. Lewis and Luther. Finally, in addition to the many points just listed that are directly relevant to more or less academic theological concerns, Žižek addresses religious topics that have become important in the popular and political spheres. On an explicit level, for example, he has addressed the problem of fundamentalism, and his work also touches on the two topics that (unfortunately) dominate popular religious debate, at least in the United States: sexuality and evolutionary theory. All of this theological material is over and above the implicit relevance that Žižek, as a philosopher, has for theological reflection simply by virtue of the historically close relationship between philosophy and theology. As mentioned, I will devote part of this chapter to exploring two areas of this implicit relevance, but I turn first to survey what theologians have thus far made of the ample material Žižek supplies them for response.

Responses from Radical Orthodoxy

Among the very first theologians to respond to Žižek's work were members of the Radical Orthodoxy movement. This school of theology originated in the United Kingdom and is named after the edited volume that first brought together many of its leading lights.[8] The movement takes its primary impetus from the work of John Milbank, who combines a strong commitment to Augustine and Aquinas with a harsh criticism of modern and postmodern thought. As a result of the critical arm of their approach, Radical Orthodox theologians tend to be much more concerned to keep up with the latest developments in European philosophy and political thought than those in other theological movements. Thus Graham Ward, one of the founders of Radical Orthodoxy, produced the first extended theological discussion of Žižek's work in his *Cities of God*,[9] which is a theological response to the city and to broader questions of contemporary social structures. In this work, Žižek's *Plague of Fantasies* serves as a counterpoint to Ward's analysis of the intertwined issues of pornography and cyberspace.

More than any specific problem, however, Radical Orthodoxy is concerned with the issue of ontology, the underlying metaphysical framework of reality. They argue that in the modern period, virtually all philosophers have embraced what they call the 'univocity of being', following on the medieval theologian Duns Scotus's claim that the word 'being' means the same thing (is univocal) when referring to God and creation. For Milbank and others, the key example of the 'univocity of being' is the philosophy of Gilles Deleuze, and so, in recent years, Radical Orthodox theologians have shown a deep interest in Alain Badiou, for whom Deleuze was a major influence. As an alternative to the modern ontology, which they regard as 'nihilistic', Radical Orthodoxy proposes a return to the *analogia entis* or 'analogy of being'. In contrast to Karl Barth's famous claim that the *analogia entis* is 'the invention of the Antichrist',[10] Radical Orthodoxy's contention is that only the synthesis of Neo-Platonism and Christianity achieved by Augustine and further developed by Aquinas can allow for a genuinely meaningful worldview, one in which God is the fullness of being and all created beings participate analogically in that fullness to the extent that they are able.[11]

Though Graham Ward's response to Žižek is based in the particular problems of cyberspace and pornography, the ultimate stake remains the establishment of an analogical worldview to displace the prevailing nihilistic univocal stance. In contrast to the conventional view of Christianity as opposed to the erotic, Ward claims that only an analogical worldview can ground a meaningful sexuality, which for him is always also a meaningful political order.[12] This is because only analogy can meaningfully sustain desire, which binds together personal relationships and political communities alike. After reading a variety of modern philosophers through this lens, Ward turns to Žižek's *Plague of Fantasies* and particularly his account of fantasy as that which both enables and prevents an encounter with the other,[13] and his argument that the true problem with virtual reality is that it collapses the symbolic order – that is, that it is not virtual enough insofar as it does not sustain the gap that is necessary for desire.[14] Ward uses Žižek's emphasis on the negative, lack and the void to place him in a series of contemporary philosophers (above all Derrida) who critique the notion of presence.[15] For Ward, however, Žižek's emphasis on negativity leaves him 'vulnerable to the criticism that the body, the material world is devalued', insofar as the emphasis falls on the symbolic order that is structured by lacks and by the Real as the primordial void.[16] In place of this nihilistic view, Ward proposes the traditional notions of Eucharistic presence and of participation in the Holy Spirit as the best ground for an authentic sexuality and community. Since *Plague of Fantasies*, Žižek has addressed at least some of these critiques with his notion of Christian love as a very bodily and material form of love, and it would be interesting to see what Ward's response would be to Žižek's more recent work. However, Žižek is only beginning to respond to the most incisive and general criticism Ward offers: 'Žižek offers critique, but no constructive move beyond critique.'[17]

The two remaining Radical Orthodox responses appear in the *Theology and the Political* collection and come from Žižek's co-editors. First, 'Metanoia: The Theological Practice of Revolution', co-authored by Creston Davis and Patrick Aaron Riches, praises the recent turn to theology among radical thinkers such as Žižek and forcefully argues that socialism 'must finally and irrevocably jettison its alliance with modernity, progressivism, and atheism', and turn instead to a theological ontology that can provide the ground for a revolutionary new order.[18] Davis and Riches respond to Žižek primarily as a way of showing the inadequacy of a dialectical ontology as opposed to an analogical one. Embracing the traditional reading of Hegel that portrays him as always swallowing up all difference into sameness, they claim that 'the Žižekian "Real"' represents 'a logical unfolding that repeats itself in absolute unproductive terms'.[19] Later they claim that Žižek's frequent move of shifting an epistemological obstacle into an ontological fault represents a 'dialectic that rejects all difference which cannot be subsumed into its own unfolding' and compare him unfavourably to Aquinas insofar as Žižek claims that the universe 'remains entirely devoid of a real cause external to itself'.[20] In my view, Davis and Riches err when they collapse Žižek into the traditional reading of Hegel, given that one of Žižek's key tasks since *Sublime Object* has been to debunk that reading and to present a Hegel who affirms difference and contingency. It is possible that Žižek has failed on this count, but if Davis and Riches believe that to be the case, they should acknowledge what Žižek is attempting to do with Hegel and make an argument that he does not succeed, rather than simply assuming a strict identity between Žižek's work and the traditional reading of Hegel. Overall, their critique of Žižek seems to me to miss its target – though I am sure Žižek would concede that his thought differs from that of Aquinas.

The final response to Žižek from the Radical Orthodoxy school is found in John Milbank's contribution to *Theology and the Political*, 'Materialism and Transcendence'. Milbank begins by claiming that postwar French Marxist thought has consistently tried to 'supply Marxism with a more adequate ontology than was contained within the writings of Marx himself'. For Milbank, Marx was essentially a reductive materialist, and so these later thinkers sought non-reductive forms of materialism that 'borrow from Platonic-Aristotelian, Idealist, and even theological thought'.[21] Clearly Žižek falls under this description, and Milbank at first groups him with Badiou due to their common rejection of 'politically correct' pluralism, which for Milbank naturally leads them to embrace Christianity as 'the religion of universalism'.[22] After a lengthy treatment of Badiou and Deleuze, Milbank turns to Žižek's approach to Christianity. He notes that for Žižek, the way to get beyond the law is not to give way to fantasy (in what Žižek calls 'perversion'), but rather to sacrifice fantasy itself. Though Milbank agrees with this notion, he detects a contradiction insofar as Žižek claims that the law is necessary to sustain desire, which Milbank appears to take as constitutive of human social links. Thus Milbank believes that no political practice can be imagined as a result of going through the fantasy: 'On this ontological basis one can imagine the gesture of revolution, but really no stable progress toward socialism, much less its stable achievement.'[23] Ultimately, Milbank claims that 'Žižek sustains the nihilism that Lenin, in a very Russian fashion, tended to add to Marxism' and characterizes Žižek as 'a mystical nihilist'.[24] Certainly Žižek, with his continual emphasis on the negative, can more fairly be characterized as a nihilist than most. Nevertheless, it seems to me that Milbank misses two key notions by which Žižek tries to escape the impasse Milbank points out: the level of drive (as opposed to desire) and the idea of the discourse of the analyst as a social link that escapes the pitfalls of ideology (or 'Law'). Milbank's critique fits well with what I've called the 'middle period' of Žižek's trajectory, but it ultimately lags behind Žižek's development in the more recent work to which Milbank is responding. At the same time, more than Davis and Riches and perhaps even Ward, Milbank is careful to respond to Žižek in his specificity without being overly quick to lump him with someone else. Beyond that, he endorses the connection with which I plan to end this chapter, namely, the idea that Žižek is practising 'a Hegelian death of God theology'.[25]

Other theological responses

The majority of theological responses from outside the Radical Orthodoxy school were prompted, perhaps unsurprisingly, by Žižek's work on Christianity. In some quarters, Žižek's turn to theology – along with the 'religious turn' in European philosophy in general and Marxism in particular – has been applauded, much as Milbank's essay commends Marxists for enriching their ontology with theological resources. For instance, the historian and social critic Eugene McCarraher, reviewing *The Puppet and the Dwarf* in the left-wing journal *In These Times*,[26] is generally enthusiastic: 'Coming as close as an atheist probably can to a bold assertion of faith, Žižek becomes the godless theologian of our time, exhibiting all the sacred foolishness of that hopeful and futile vocation.' Nevertheless, for McCarraher, 'Žižek's Pauline theology collapses because, to put it squarely, it does not assert the exterior reality of God, on which Christian joy and political commitment must inevitably rest.' More specifically, McCarraher believes that Žižek's rejection of the resurrection of the body undercuts any genuine hope. A similar structure can be found in

Paul J. Griffiths' essay 'Christ and Critical Theory' in the right-wing Roman Catholic organ *First Things*.[27] A survey of recent work by various thinkers, Griffiths' essay is most sympathetic toward Žižek, in large part because Žižek is much more willing to engage directly in theological reasoning without limiting himself to a reading of a particular religious text. Nevertheless, Žižek still comes up short because he does not regard the Roman Catholic Church as the 'institutional form appropriate to the community brought into being by the Holy Spirit' – and indeed, for Griffiths Žižek fails even to offer any good reason not to embrace the church. In my view, such a claim ignores the fact that Žižek's goal in his work on Christianity is in part to develop a concept of a social form that would escape the fetishization of institutions and also ignores Žižek's strident critique of actual existing Christianity, especially its Catholic form. In any case, with due allowance for their radically different political commitments, both of these authors' arguments – and those of Žižek's Radical Orthodox critics as well – come down to the same basic point: it is good that Žižek is interested in Christianity, but he is not Christian enough.

By contrast, the Anabaptist thinker Gerald Biesecker-Mast, in his essay 'Slavoj Žižek, the Fragile Absolute, and the Anabaptist Subject',[28] more or less brackets Žižek's theological claims. Instead, he commends Žižek's account of the guilt-ridden nature of much Christian practice and his privileging of Jewish 'legalism'. Against certain Anabaptist thinkers who claim that Anabaptist churches have been hindered by their lack of 'spirituality', Biesecker-Mast argues that Anabaptist 'legalism' is actually more psychologically healthy than other versions of Christianity. Beyond that, he sees in Žižek's ethics an echo of the Anabaptist stance of radical renunciation – including the renunciation of a rich 'spiritual life'. Thus, while a conservative Roman Catholic finds Žižek's critique of the institutional church unacceptable, at least one heir of the Radical Reformation finds in Žižek's work an affirmation of his community's distinctive stance.

Two further responses can be found in the recent edited volume entitled *Latin American Liberation Theology: The Next Generation*.[29] Manuel J. Mejido's contribution embraces Žižek's work as a way of getting beyond postmodern relativism by using psychoanalysis as a grounding for the social scientific approach that has been so central to Latin American liberation theology. In particular, Mejido believes Žižek's approach 'provides the possibility of . . . therapeutically going beyond the naturalization of global liberal-democratic capitalism'.[30] By contrast, Nelson Maldonado-Torres pairs Žižek with Milbank, arguing that both display 'an exclusivist attitude, resistance to dialogue, and reliance on old Christian prejudices'. For Maldonado-Torres, Žižek's 'new Marxist orthodoxy' is every bit as toxic as the orthodox Christianity with which he allies it.[31] He critiques (rightly in my view) Žižek's one-sided presentation of Buddhism in *The Puppet and the Dwarf* and argues that Žižek also marginalizes Judaism as 'a transitory but utterly necessary moment'. As a result, 'Žižek criticizes Christian anti-Semitism with an epistemological framework that promotes, if it is not itself, anti-Semitic' – by which he seems to mean that Žižek holds to the supercessionist position that is at the root of anti-Semitism.[32] Overall, Maldonado-Torres holds that Žižek remains within the same Western framework as the liberalism he opposes, resulting in 'the *recolonization* of entire areas of thought and the suspension of dialogue'.[33] In short, Žižek is *too* Christian.

Representatives of other liberation theologies have not yet responded to Žižek in print, at least to the best of my knowledge. Given Žižek's notoriety, it seems most reasonable to interpret this silence not as a sign that members of such groups have not been keeping up, but rather as an unspoken decision that their energies would be better spent elsewhere. Feminist theologians, for example, already too often face an uphill battle in legitimating their work in contemporary academic and ecclesiastical circles and in relation to the major figures in the tradition, essentially all of whom are of a patriarchal bent. Since Žižek's work is so saturated with gendered language and sexist clichés and since he displays such a patronizing attitude toward feminism in general, feminist theologians may well view Žižek as a potential opponent – an opponent they would not gain much by defeating. On the other hand, black theologians may be disinclined to devote much attention to Žižek because he so seldom addresses the black experience. Aside from a brief discussion of Malcolm X in *Tarrying with the Negative* and a lengthier engagement with Toni Morrison's *Beloved* in *The Fragile Absolute*,[34] African Americans are almost totally absent from Žižek's work, despite his focus on American culture. This is even more the case for the other minority groups who have more recently begun self-consciously developing their own theological traditions.

Finally, I turn to two theologians who are working outside the boundaries of Christian orthodoxy: John D. Caputo and Clayton Crockett. Perhaps most famous for his work *The Prayers and Tears of Jacques Derrida*, which argued for a religious reading of Derrida's deconstruction, Caputo has recently turned more explicitly toward theology with *The Weakness of God: A Theology of the Event*.[35] His primary goal is to advance an idea of God as an event that must be thought in terms of weakness rather than power,[36] and in its basic outlines, such a project seems as though it could at least enter into a productive dialogue with Žižek's work on Christianity. Nevertheless, most of Caputo's remarks on Žižek are negative, though he does little to clarify what he thinks is wrong with Žižek's positions.[37] A much more sympathetic account is found in Clayton Crockett's *Interstices of the Sublime*, which uses Lacanian psychoanalysis to challenge traditional theology. Unlike most of the theologians addressed in this chapter, then, Crockett focuses his attention on Žižek's theoretical work rather than his thoughts on Christianity. Though he spends some time with the accounts of sexual difference and of subjectivity from *Tarrying with the Negative*, Crockett's lengthiest engagement with Žižek comes in two chapters on the concept of creation *ex nihilo*. There, Crockett brings together Žižek's reading of Schelling from *The Indivisible Remainder* and Tillich's two dissertations on Schelling, interweaving both with a reading of Lacan, leading to the conclusion that the task of theology is 'the creation of theological ideas – out of nothing'.[38] Ultimately Crockett finds Tillich's approach more convincing, but his reading of Žižek is detailed and sympathetic, truly putting Žižek's ideas to work for theology. Hopefully Crockett will be only the first of many theologians to put aside the task of simply responding to Žižek's books on Christianity with a yes or a no and turn instead to the philosophical trajectory that undergirds his work on theology.

Theological responses

Žižek's 'method of correlation'

Following up on Crockett's linking of the two through their work on Schelling, I would like to draw a connection between Tillich and Žižek's respective methods of engaging culture. In the first volume of his *Systematic Theology*, Tillich lays out the 'method of correlation', which he claims has been the implicit method of systematic theology throughout its history, especially when theology has had an apologetic goal. Though he lays out three forms of correlation, the most important is that 'between concepts denoting the human and those denoting the divine', the latter of which Tillich usually calls 'symbols'.[39] The correlation between the human and divine is that between a question and its answer. The human situation, when taken seriously in its full depth, necessarily leads human beings to ask ultimate, existential questions – to the point that Tillich can say, 'Man [*sic*] is the question he asks about himself, before any question has been formulated.'[40] God's revelation provides the answer to those questions by means of religious symbols corresponding to those questions. By this, Tillich does not mean that revelation is a final deposit of 'one size fits all' answers. Rather, God's answers, in order to be intelligible, must respond to the concrete questions human beings are asking at any given historical moment.

Thus the task of theology is twofold: 'it makes an analysis of the human situation out of which the existential questions arise, and it demonstrates that the symbols used in the Christian message are the answers to these questions'.[41] The first task is most fundamentally a philosophical one, consisting in analysing the human situation and the questions implied in human existence. In order to perform this analysis, the theologian necessarily makes use of philosophy, but also 'poetry, drama, the novel, therapeutic psychology, and sociology' – in other words, the entire range of what is normally called 'high culture' and the human sciences.[42] The philosophical analysis of existence is an absolutely necessary step if theology is to remain relevant and convincing and, more fundamentally, to fulfil its basic duty. After all, 'man [*sic*] cannot receive answers to questions he never has asked', and the theologian works in confidence that Christianity's symbols provide the best answers to those questions.

Žižek does not seem to have laid out an explicit theoretical justification for his use of popular culture – in fact, most often he has said that incorporating it into his theoretical work simply gives him an excuse to indulge himself. Nevertheless, I believe that his practice can best be interpreted as a variation on Tillich's method of correlation, one that may serve as a productive model for theological engagement with culture. The emphasis falls overwhelmingly on the side of discerning the existential questions at the heart of a given historical situation. In this regard, Žižek's method is both wider-ranging and more detailed. Tillich limits himself to the most serious cultural productions and the findings of philosophy and the social sciences. While Žižek certainly includes such sources in his cultural analysis, he is most famous for his love of 'low' culture – most notably film, but also television commercials, consumer products and jokes of varying degrees of vulgarity and offensiveness. This broad range stems from Žižek's theory of ideology critique. Since everything outside of the coercive powers of the state – down to the bare level of language itself – falls under the category of 'ideology', essentially every cultural product is within Žižek's purview. As indicated in the first two chapters, for Žižek, ideology is an inherently contradictory realm, and so just as the goal of Tillich's analysis is to elicit existential questions, the goal of Žižek's ideology critique is to expose those contradictions. In concrete terms, that means showing that the cultural products under consideration reflect the underlying ideological contradictions of society.

For the critic of ideology, then, everything is a potential example, even the most obviously 'incorrect' clichés. From Tillich's point of view, examining the unthinking ideas of the crowd may seem to be a failure to take the task of analysing human existence seriously enough, but for Žižek, by contrast, '"Clichés" should . . . be taken extremely seriously.'[43] To use a previous example, it's not enough simply to laugh off the idea that Mexican immigrants are lazy or that they are 'stealing our jobs'. The real question is what has allowed those two contradictory ideas to become common currency simultaneously. The result of Žižek's apparently 'unserious' approach is that he ends up treating cultural phenomena in much greater detail than Tillich ever does. At times, Žižek's prolific range of references threatens to turn him into a kind of inverse of Tillich: where Tillich gives his readers a clear conceptual scheme with virtually no examples, Žižek gives so many examples that they can obscure the

Theological responses

concepts that inform them. Nevertheless, Žižek's extremely wide net can serve as an example for theologians who still mainly limit their cultural analysis to philosophy and literature.

So as not to be completely out of the spirit of Žižek, it seems appropriate to give a concrete example of his cultural analysis. Although Žižek has devoted much of his attention to the films of highly regarded directors like Alfred Hitchcock and David Lynch, perhaps the best example to use in his context is his analysis of a series that all but the most die-hard fans regard as bad: the *Star Wars* prequels. Žižek does not dissent from the consensus on the films' quality, but his analysis in *The Parallax View* aims to uncover why the series failed. He begins by noting that George Lucas himself drew a parallel between the shift from the Republic to the Empire and the shift from Anakin Skywalker to Darth Vader, but failed to follow through on that parallel in any coherent way in the films themselves.[44] The result is that the 'political connotations of the *Star Wars* universe are multiple and inconsistent', which is precisely what gives the series its mythic power:

> A political *myth* proper is not so much a narrative with some determinate political meaning but, rather, an empty container of a multitude of inconsistent, even mutually exclusive, meanings – it is wrong to ask 'But what does this political myth really mean?', since its 'meaning' is precisely to serve as the container for a multitude of meanings.[45]

For Žižek, the incoherence on the political level reflects the uncertain moment in which we find ourselves, where the traditional form of the nation-state is weakening and where the United States seems in many ways to be on the brink of transforming itself into a global empire. As in the *Star Wars* universe, here the Republic and the Empire are ultimately the same entity, but there is a failure of nerve when it comes to facing up to this fact: 'the bad Empire is not out there; it emerges through the very way we, the "good guys," fight the bad Empire, the enemy out there – in today's "war on terror," the problem is what this war will turn the USA into'.[46]

This political incoherence is reflected in the figure of Anakin Skywalker/Darth Vader. Žižek's analysis of this character provides

143

perhaps the clearest example of Žižek's equivalent to the second half of Tillich's method of correlation: the theological answer to the existential questions of the day. First, Žižek notes that despite the audience's awareness that he is going to become the evil Darth Vader, Anakin has many Christ-like features, not least of which is the implied virgin birth. Echoing the parallel he draws in his works on Christianity between the present world of 'perversion' and the paganism of ancient Rome, Žižek sees the parallel between Christ and Darth Vader as completely appropriate: 'Since the ideological universe of *Star Wars* is the New Age pagan universe, it is quite logical that its central figure of Evil should echo Christ – within the pagan horizon, the Event of Christ is the ultimate scandal.'[47] Second, for Žižek, the films fail on their own terms to provide a compelling account of Anakin's shift to the Dark Side. Whereas he argues that Anakin 'should have become a monster out of his very excessive attachment to seeing Evil everywhere and fighting it', in point of fact Anakin comes across as a fundamentally weak character who is simply drawn to evil by the fascination of power. Thus while the films want to paint Anakin as an eruption of radical evil, in reality they present a fairly banal tale of someone seduced by a combination of pride and self-pity.

Nevertheless, once the transition to the Dark Side is completed, Žižek sees Anakin as adopting a properly ethical stance. In his final duel with Obi-wan Kenobi, Anakin is offered one last chance to return to the path of good before Obi-wan kills him – nevertheless, on the model of the 'choice of the worst', Anakin refuses: 'in an act of defiance that cannot but appear uncannily ethical, [he] courageously remain[s] faithful to [his] choice out of principle, not on account of the promise of any material or spiritual profit'.[48] For Žižek, such a gesture is, on the formal level, fundamentally Christian, and he even ends his section on the *Star Wars* prequels with an assertion of 'the *literal* truth of Lacan's statement according to which [theologians] are the only true materialists'.[49] Thus one can say that Žižek's equivalent to Tillich's 'theological answer' is also 'theological', but in Žižek's idiosyncratic sense of the term – that is, focused on redeeming lost opportunities and on the paradoxically ethical 'choice of the worst' that, echoing the psychoanalytic cure, takes place at the 'theological' level of drive.

Theological responses

Žižek and tradition

In the course of Žižek's trajectory, the exposure of ideological contradictions that serves as his equivalent for Tillich's search for existential questions has been more thoroughly developed, but in his more recent work, the 'theological response' has become an increasingly urgent task. A significant portion of this 'theological' work has also been theological in the direct sense, namely, his work on Christianity. Though I have tried to show that the books on Christianity represent a decisive turning-point in his development, it is nevertheless clear that his real personal investment is in a 'theological' approach to another tradition: revolutionary Marxism. In Žižek's view, this tradition has its roots in Christianity,[50] but the modern revolutionary tradition is more directly 'his', not only because he spent much of his life under Communist rule, but also because of his uncompromising commitment to the political Left. Thus, in this section, I propose Žižek as a potential model for theologians, demonstrating what it means to be loyal to, and at the same time take responsibility for, a tradition.

Žižek is candid about the major problems facing anyone who advocates any kind of return to the revolutionary Marxist tradition. Not only was its primary concrete outcome, the Soviet bloc, an oppressive regime that caused death and suffering on an unimaginable scale, but it was also a clear failure – in place of a dynamic socialist utopia, it resulted in a bureaucratic dictatorship that eventually collapsed. Thus the only serious alternative to capitalism turned out to be both unappealing and ineffective, and now Communism only survives in a handful of small countries and an increasingly capitalistic China. Žižek makes no effort to whitewash either the terrors of Stalinism or the very real oppression of the post-Stalinist era, and in fact he has very little patience for nostalgic Western Marxists who are scornful of the Eastern European countries' embrace of liberal democracy and capitalism. He frankly admits that things went horribly wrong and that any thought of a return to Real Socialism is obviously out of the question – but he nevertheless insists on the absolute necessity of moving beyond a simple rejection of Communism and undertaking a detailed analysis of precisely *how* it went wrong.

Žižek rejects out of hand one very common rhetorical tactic on the left: the attempt to create a narrative of a fall. The options for such a narrative are many – Lenin betrayed Marx's insights by starting the revolution in the wrong time and place, Stalin betrayed Lenin, it was all going fine until Mao came along and wrecked everything, etc.[51] Such tactics are of course pervasive in Christian discourse as well: Jesus was a great liberator, but Paul screwed everything up; Paul understood the core of the gospel, but the development of early Catholicism obscured it; early Christianity was doing just fine until they sold out to Constantine; Luther reactivated the core of the gospel, but the subsequent institutionalization of Protestantism betrayed his insights; Christian civilization was going great until Luther came along and undermined Christian unity, etc., etc., etc. In contrast to this logic, Žižek insists that:

> There is no opposition here, the Fall is to be inscribed into the very origins. (To put it even more pointedly, such a search for the intruder who infected the original model and set in motion its degeneration cannot but reproduce the logic of anti-Semitism.) What this means is that, even if – or, rather, especially if – one submits the Marxist past to a ruthless critique, one has first to acknowledge it as 'one's own,' taking full responsibility for it, not to comfortably get rid of the 'bad' turn of the things by way of attributing it to a foreign intruder.[52]

In Žižek's context, that means dispensing once and for all with the idea that Marx is perfect and that all the oppression of Real Socialism is a betrayal of Marx's fundamental insights. Instead, Žižek argues that 'as Marxists, in the interests of our fidelity to Marx's work, we should identify Marx's mistake'.[53] Marx's critique of political economy is still a powerful tool and, for Žižek, is in fact more relevant than ever, but

> Marx's fundamental mistake was to conclude, from these insights, that a new, higher social order (Communism) is possible, an order that would not only maintain but even raise to a higher degree, and effectively release, the potential of the self-increasing spiral of productivity in which capitalism, on account of its inherent obstacle/contradic-

tion, is thwarted again and again by socially destructive economic crises.⁵⁴

In other words, Marx himself betrayed Marxism through the fantasy that a utopian society could automatically be generated out of capitalism – the betrayal that led to Real Socialism is in fact one of Marx's central concepts. For a Marxist, this critique is a radical move, approximately the equivalent of a Christian claiming that Jesus got something fundamentally wrong.⁵⁵

Instead of simply returning to Marx in the sense of reasserting the correctness of his analysis, Žižek proposes an approach that is central to his reappropriation of the revolutionary tradition as a whole: Kierkegaard's notion of a non-identical *repetition*. In the case of Marx, Žižek believes that the fantasy of Communism was still stuck within the framework of capitalism, insofar as it took for granted the desirability of continual growth and dynamism. The task then becomes to discover 'how to *repeat* the Marxist "critique of political economy" without the utopian-ideological notion of Communism as its inherent standard'.⁵⁶ Such a move would mean conceptualizing a much more radical break with capitalism than Real Socialism, which basically amounted to an inefficient state-run capitalism. Another example of the same basic logic is his proposal to 'repeat Lenin'. In his introduction to *Revolution at the Gates*, a collection of Lenin's writings from 1917, Žižek clarifies the Lenin he wishes to return to:

> 'Lenin' is not the nostalgic name for old dogmatic certainty; quite the contrary, *the* Lenin who is to be retrieved is the Lenin whose fundamental experience was that of being thrown into a catastrophic new constellation [specifically, the capitulation of the international worker's movement to the nationalism leading to the First World War]⁵⁷ in which the old co-ordinates proved useless, and who was thus compelled to reinvent Marxism – take his acerbic remark apropos of some new problem: 'About this, Marx and Engels said not a word.'⁵⁸

Thus the point is not to return to the specific *content* of Lenin's thought and work, but '*repeating*, in the present worldwide conditions, the Leninist gesture of reinventing the revolutionary project'.[59] In both cases, what is to be preserved and non-identically repeated is fundamentally a negative gesture: critiquing capitalism, rejecting the dogmatic certainty of other Marxists who thought nothing had changed. By isolating the explosive energy of that moment from the past, the contemporary revolutionary can attempt to redeem it.

The corollary to Žižek's attempt to isolate the moments of genuine liberatory potential in the revolutionary heritage is his effort to discern how things went so terribly wrong. The overwhelming focus of this effort is Stalinism, to which he has devoted an increasing amount of attention over the course of his trajectory, almost to the point of obsession. His first step in diagnosing the problem is asserting at least some kind of continuity between Stalinism and, not just Marxism, but the Enlightenment tradition as a whole. He rejects the idea that fascism and Stalinism are simply equivalent, and, in a variety of works, he has detailed his reasons. For example, horrible as the Stalinist show-trials were, the bare fact of having a trial provides some connection to a just society — whereas the idea of a Jew being put on trial under Nazism is simply nonsensical. Additionally, in popular culture, Communism is not subject to the same absolute taboo as Nazism, showing at least a tacit acknowledgment of the liberatory intent of Communism, even in the light of its betrayal. More directly, Stalin shows his connection to Lenin in his ruthless determination to transform Russian society, as shown in the process of collectivizing agriculture. This connection to the Leninist moment means that there are at least some potentials in Stalinism that can be redeemed, while fascism is simply an unredeemable horror. For Žižek, therefore, claiming an equivalence between fascism and Stalinism always means silently favouring fascism, which means foreclosing the possibility of any revolutionary change.[60] Arguing that Stalinism is minimally 'better' than fascism is hardly a ringing endorsement, of course, and Žižek's diagnosis of what went wrong is essentially that Stalinism was 'perverse'. Relying on the 'big Other' of Historical Necessity — a concept inherited directly from Marx and Engels — the Stalinist subject is able to justify even the most heinous crimes as necessary for the establishment of the Communist utopia. (In opposition to this perverse stance, Žižek advocates a Leninist 'revolutionary *act* not covered by the big Other'.⁶¹)

To give some indication of how a Žižekian approach to the Christian tradition might work, I have chosen one of the many ambiguous figures from the Christian tradition: Clement of Alexandria. Clement is usually classed among the apologists, who supposedly 'introduced' the Greek philosophical concepts that it has for a long time been fashionable to blame for the failure of Christianity to live up to its promise.⁶² If one sets aside the possibility of a fall narrative where Clement and his peers 'sold out' Christianity, however, it becomes clear that many of the aspects that are most appealing in Clement's vision of Christian community – the emphasis on learning for all members, the inclusion of women as peers – are a direct result of his understanding, and perhaps even reinvention, of Christianity as a continuation and radicalization of the Greek philosophical tradition. Where the Greeks held that certain people were born to be slaves and were generally sceptical of the ability of women to practise philosophy, Clement asserted that Christianity was the superior philosophy because it was able to induct *everyone* into the philosophical lifestyle, which meant above all a life freed from the fear of death. Thus, even though Clement and others' use of Platonic philosophical concepts had some undesirable effects, both in his own work and that of later generations, one could perhaps do worse than to 'repeat' Clement's daring rearticulation of the key Christian concepts of radical universalism and martyrdom in a new language and situation.

Religionless Christianity and the death of God

Having indicated two ways in which Žižek's non-theological work might be relevant to theological reflection – namely, in his approach to culture and to the tradition in which he stands – I will conclude by returning one last time to his work on Christianity. I have already attempted to demonstrate the decisive role that his theological engagement plays in his overall development and have noted some early responses from theologians, but here I hope to show that Žižek poses a profound challenge to theology, a challenge that Milbank's remark about Žižek's 'Hegelian death of God theology'[63] only hints at. This challenge is not unique to Žižek, but stems rather from his uncanny echoing of two of the most important and controversial theologians of the twentieth century: Dietrich Bonhoeffer and Thomas J. J. Altizer. Though he displays no knowledge of Altizer at all and only a superficial familiarity with Bonhoeffer,[64] Žižek nonetheless seems to me to have 'independently discovered' their central insights, and as such his notoriety may provide an opportunity to return again to certain strains of radical theological thought that have been neglected in recent years – that is, to 'repeat' them in a non-identical way.

As a result of the remarkable variety of his work and eventfulness of his tragically all-too-brief life, Bonhoeffer is many things to many people: the heroic martyr killed for his resistance to the Nazis, the student of nonviolent resistance who was nonetheless compelled to participate in an assassination plot against Hitler,[65] the critic of 'cheap grace' well loved by conservative Christians in particular. Here, however, I would like to focus on the Bonhoeffer of the *Letters and Papers from Prison*,[66] where he confronts the possibility of a radical eclipse of religion in the Western world and asks what it would mean to develop a form of Christianity that would do 'without religion, i.e., without the temporally conditioned presuppositions of metaphysics, inwardness, and so on'.[67] His answer, sketched only in its barest outlines, is a 'religionless Christianity' that would discover a way to speak 'in a "secular" way about "God"' and would regard itself 'as belonging wholly to this world'.[68] Such a Christianity would take seriously the fact that the movement 'towards the autonomy of man [sic]' has essentially been completed, so that now 'man has learnt to deal with himself in all questions of importance without recourse to the "working hypothesis" called "God"'.[69] With regard to the Bible, a 'religionless' approach means, in one sense, rejecting the demythologizing approach that attempts to trim away the aspects of the biblical text that no longer seem credible to modern people, but in another sense, radicalizing that very approach:

> My view is that the full content, including the 'mythological' concepts, must be kept – the New Testament is not a mythological clothing of a universal truth; the mythology

Theological responses

(resurrection, etc.) is the thing itself – but the concepts must be interpreted in such a way as not to make religion a precondition of faith (cf. Paul and circumcision).[70]

Bonhoeffer himself does not offer any concrete examples of this 'religionless' reading of the Bible, but Žižek's approach follows its basic outlines, and perhaps more importantly, Žižek's understanding of the ultimate meaning of the Christian story is strikingly similar to Bonhoeffer's:

> Before God and with God we live without God. God lets himself be pushed out of the world on the cross. He is weak and powerless in the world, and that is precisely the way, the only way, in which he is with us and helps us . . . Man's religiosity makes him look in his distress to the power of God in the world: God is the *deus ex machina*. The Bible directs man to God's powerlessness and suffering: only the suffering God can help.[71]

Not only must scripture be interpreted in a 'religionless' way – just as for Žižek, a proper understanding of the New Testament is one that directly frees us from religion. Both also share the notion that the advent of the 'secular' modern world opens up the space for a recovery of this authentic message of Christianity.

Altizer is best known for his role in the 'death of God' controversy of the 1960s, which resulted in the famous *Time* magazine cover asking 'Is God Dead?', and became a key inspiration for later theologians such as Mark C. Taylor and Don Cupitt. In *The Gospel of Christian Atheism*,[72] which laid out the basic position that he would develop over the course of many books in subsequent decades, Altizer cites Bonhoeffer's idea of 'religionless Christianity' with approval, but his position is more radical. Where Bonhoeffer argues that the Christian God 'wins power and space in the world by his weakness',[73] Altizer claims that God fully emptied himself into Christ, such that in the cross of Christ, God did not just display weakness, but actually *died*:

> The death of God in Christ is an inevitable consequence of the movement of God into the world, of Spirit into flesh,

and the actualization of the death of God in the totality of experience is a decisive sign of the continuing and forward movement of the divine process, as it continues to negate its particular and given expressions, by moving ever more fully into the depths of the profane.[74]

Here one perhaps finds a precursor to Žižek's more direct claim that in Christ, God 'freely *identified himself with his own shit*'.[75] More broadly, Altizer shares Žižek's view of Christianity as the religion of atheism and of the actual existing church as a betrayal of the true meaning of the gospel. This similarity stems to a large extent from overlapping sources. Both Žižek and Altizer draw their notion of God's self-emptying into the incarnate Christ from Hegel's philosophy of religion. Additionally, Altizer's privileging of Nietzsche can be seen as parallel to Žižek's use of psychoanalysis, given the widely acknowledged affinity between Nietzsche and Freud. The key difference, however, is in the 'third leg' of their respective projects: where Žižek turns to the tradition of revolutionary Marxism, Altizer draws on the apocalyptic vision found in many of the great figures of modern literature, above all William Blake and James Joyce. While Altizer believes that the death of God and his self-emptying into the world has political consequences, which he names with the Joycean phrase 'Here comes everybody', his lack of any concrete political reference point leaves him unable to give an account of how something worthy of the name of 'Here comes everybody' might come about. By contrast, Žižek, perhaps due to his grounding in the revolutionary Marxist tradition, has been able to envision at least the first steps toward a future of 'Here comes everybody'. His notion of the Holy Spirit or discourse of the analyst as a social grouping that is not grounded in the big Other but nonetheless has some particularity provides a potential 'lever' for a global transformation. Thus one could perhaps understand the sequence Bonhoeffer–Altizer–Žižek in dialectical terms. Altizer rejects Bonhoeffer's desire for continuity with the existing Christian church, but he can only rush to the opposite pole of identifying the true object of God's action as 'the world' at large. Žižek discards the frame of church vs. world, which allows him to envision a new form of collectivity that would non-identically repeat the 'Holy Spirit' that flowed out of the death of God on the cross.

Theological responses

This 'advance' should not, however, be understood as rendering Altizer simply obsolete. Altizer is able to develop the notion of the death of God and the link between the advent of Christianity and the advent of modernity in considerably greater depth than Žižek, in large part because of the 'fourth leg' of his project: the history of religions. In place of Žižek's potshots against Buddhism, for example, Altizer provides a depth of insight into Eastern religions that advances the uniqueness of Christianity much more convincingly. That said, Žižek's own 'fourth leg', namely popular culture, points toward what is arguably the most important difference between his work and Altizer's, even beyond the question of politics: the question of humour. Žižek is famous for his use of jokes, while Altizer's work (and, for that matter, Bonhoeffer's) is pervaded by a grave seriousness. This difference is perhaps partly one of temperament, but in his recent work, Žižek has insisted on the indissoluble link between Christianity and comedy, asking, 'is there anything more comical than Incarnation, this ridiculous overlapping of the Highest and the Lowest, the coincidence of God, creator of the universe, and a miserable man?'[76] This is not simply a light-hearted comedy, however, but a comedy that follows after a degradation – in technical terms, a subjective destitution – so thoroughgoing that the stance of tragic dignity is simply no longer available.[77] In Altizer's work, there is a pervasive sense of a man bravely facing up to the death of God, which is experienced as a real loss, a tragic loss. Žižek insists that the death of God means the impossibility of maintaining such a tragic stance – that is to say, the necessity of despairing even of despair itself. Yet this choice of what is 'even worse' than despair paradoxically opens up the realm of the comic.

Altizer is hardly alone in his lack of humour, and, in fact, a certain humourlessness could be said to dominate the entire Christian tradition. For the many theologians whose work is totally devoid of humour, there is implicit in Žižek's work a simple but potentially devastating critique: that they have somehow managed to '*miss the joke* of Christianity'.[78] Certainly there are exceptions, including the two theologians who are most important for Žižek's work: Kierkegaard and Chesterton. Extrapolating somewhat, I would suggest Martin Luther, Karl Barth and Mary Daly as potential candidates for theologians who 'got the joke', and perhaps even Jesus himself, a man whose use of irony and indirection is consistently underplayed by both dour conservatives and earnest liberals. What these figures share in common, among themselves and with Žižek, is a certain lack of fit within institutions and a corresponding lack of the dignity conferred by such institutions – Jesus preaching on the hillside and making himself a target of political and religious elites alike; Luther condemned by the church but never quite trying to create a separate movement; Kierkegaard posing as a socialite and publishing under bizarre pseudonyms; Chesterton writing theology after gaining notoriety as a detective novelist; Barth devoting much of his labour as a pastor to organizing workers and then becoming the foremost theologian in the world without ever receiving a doctorate; Daly piling up degrees in order to serve an institution she knew would never recognize her and extolling the 'sisterhood of man'. Even in the case of Altizer, there is a certain performative humour in declaring the death of God on national television and spending the next four decades and more writing obsessively about God. Compared to the majority of theologians, these figures had nothing to lose, and so they could afford, in a certain sense, to laugh – and gained a new kind of unauthorized authority through that laughter.

Discouraging, then, as Žižek's call for Christianity to abandon its institutional identity may be for the increasing number of theologians who insist that theology must be of and for 'the church', such a call is hardly unprecedented and in fact stands in a long counter-tradition. The question that prompted this book was of course why Žižek is doing *theology*, and I have done my best to answer it. Now, however, from the theological perspective, perhaps the most important question still remains: why is *Žižek* doing theology? Why is the role formerly played by internal critics who had somehow 'fallen out' of the institutional structure now being played by an outsider?

I leave the question unanswered as an exercise for the reader.

Notes

Introduction: A materialist theology?
1. Slavoj Žižek, *The Sublime Object of Ideology* (New York: Verso, 1989). In perhaps the most prominent example, Judith Butler devoted an entire chapter of the follow-up to her hugely influential book *Gender Trouble* to a critique of *Sublime Object*. See Judith Butler, 'Arguing with the Real', in *Bodies That Matter: On the Discursive Limits of 'Sex'* (New York: Routledge, 1993).
2. Slavoj Žižek, *Welcome to the Desert of the Real: Five Essays on September 11 and Related Dates* (New York: Verso, 2002). This essay appeared online in several iterations before its publication in book form, both on Žižek's website (http://www.lacan.com) and on various academic listservs – one of those earlier versions was the first text of Žižek's that I ever read.
3. Slavoj Žižek, *The Ticklish Subject: The Absent Center of Political Ontology* (New York: Verso, 1999); Alain Badiou, *Saint Paul: The Foundation of Universalism*, trans. Ray Brassier (Stanford: Stanford University Press, 2003).
4. Slavoj Žižek, *The Fragile Absolute: Or, Why is the Christian Legacy Worth Fighting For?* (New York: Verso, 2000); *On Belief* (New York: Routledge, 2001); *The Puppet and the Dwarf: The Perverse Core of Christianity* (Cambridge: MIT Press, 2003); *The Parallax View* (Cambridge: MIT Press, 2006).
5. *Puppet and the Dwarf*, 6. In this, as in all quotations from Žižek in this book, italics are in the original.
6. In retrospect, it seems clear that a regime that would regard such a position as a kind of *punishment* for an academic could not long endure.
7. For a helpful account of the work of the Slovenian Lacanians, see Ernesto Laclau's preface to *Sublime Object*. Several of Žižek's friends from Slovenia have also published works in English, including Mladen Dolar, Renata Salecl and Alenka Zupančič.
8. This brief sketch of Žižek's life relies primarily on the biographical summary in Tony Myers' *Slavoj Žižek* (New York: Routledge, 2003), which Myers has also made available online at <http://www.lacan.com/zizekchro.htm>. (Incidentally, my own research into the curious institution of a four-person presidency reveals that Slovenia maintained it for only a brief period after independence and has since switched to the more traditional one-person presidency.)
9. A tendency about which Žižek complains in 'With Defenders Like These, Who Needs Attackers?', in *The Truth of Žižek*, ed. Paul Bowman and Richard Stamp (New York: Continuum, 2007), 199. Those with a taste for polemic should make a point of reading this harsh response to his critics.
10. In the introductory literature, Ian Parker's *Slavoj Žižek: A Critical Introduction*

(Sterling, VA: Pluto Press, 2004) is the chief example of this tendency, arguing that Žižek's use of his sources is unsystematic and occasional. Sarah Kay's *Žižek: A Critical Introduction* (Malden, MA: Blackwell, 2003) is more agnostic on the question of Žižek's systematicity.

11. Simon Jarvis, 'Slavoj Žižek, *The Parallax View* (review)', *The Liberal* (October/November 2006), 38–9, <http://www.theliberal.co.uk/issue_9/reviews/nf_jarvis_9.html> (accessed 28 September 2007).
12. Rex Butler's *Slavoj Žižek: Live Theory* (New York: Continuum, 2005) is an attempt to demonstrate that there is a 'Žižekian' system. Jodi Dean's *Žižek's Politics* (New York: Routledge, 2006), which at the time of this writing was the only work on Žižek devoted to one particular topic aside from the present volume, also presupposes an underlying system in Žižek's work and explicates his political stances in light of that system.
13. Slavoj Žižek, *For They Know Not What They Do: Enjoyment as a Political Factor*, 2nd edn (New York: Verso, 2002), 101.
14. *For They Know Not*, 154. For the benefit of those familiar with Wittgenstein's work, he proposes that the late work *On Certainty* represents a further stage beyond the *Philosophical Investigations*.
15. Even the film example I choose is non-representative. Instead of examining his pervasive use of Alfred Hitchcock and David Lynch, I have selected the films that are most tied up with his analysis of Christianity: the *Star Wars* prequels. (See Chapter 5.)
16. Here I differ with Jodi Dean, whose desire to show that Žižek has been a consistent critic of liberalism leads her to misread the many arguments in favour of democracy in *Sublime Object* as critiques of democracy. See *Žižek's Politics*, 103–4.
17. Slavoj Žižek, *Tarrying with the Negative: Kant, Hegel, and the Critique of Ideology* (Durham: Duke University Press, 1993).
18. Slavoj Žižek, *The Indivisible Remainder: An Essay on Schelling and Related Matters* (New York: Verso, 1996).
19. The work of assessing Žižek's use of his sources is of course very important and necessary, but, in my view, the more important task in the context of an introductory work is simply to present what those sources mean *for Žižek*, what Žižek is doing with them. Those who prefer a more critical approach may wish to supplement this book with Ian Parker's *Slavoj Žižek: A Critical Introduction*, which is organized around an evaluation of Žižek's use of his primary three sources.
20. *Sublime Object*, 7.
21. *Ticklish Subject*, 74 (my ellipses).
22. *Puppet and the Dwarf*, 102.
23. *Puppet and the Dwarf*, 103.
24. *Puppet and the Dwarf*, 103 (my ellipses).
25. *Puppet and the Dwarf*, 103 (my ellipses).
26. *For They Know Not*, 30.
27. *For They Know Not*, 204.
28. Dean, *Žižek's Politics*, 139–41.
29. Dean, *Žižek's Politics*, 141.
30. See G. W. F. Hegel, *Phenomenology of Spirit*, trans. A. V. Miller (Oxford:

Clarendon Press, 1977), *Science of Logic*, trans. A. V. Miller (New York: Humanities Press, 1969), *Encyclopedia Logic*, trans. T. F. Geraets, W. A. Suchting and H. S. Harris (Indianapolis: Hackett, 1991), and either *Lectures on the Philosophy of Religion*, 3 vols, ed. Peter Hodgson (Berkeley: University of California Press, 1984–87) or *Lectures on the Philosophy of Religion: The Lectures of 1827*, ed. Peter Hodgson (Berkeley: University of California Press, 1988); Alexander Kojève, *Introduction to the Reading of Hegel*, ed. Allan Bloom, trans. James H. Nichols, Jr (New York: Basic Books, 1969); Stephen Houlgate, *Introduction to Hegel: Freedom, Truth, and History*, 2nd edn (Malden, MA: Blackwell, 2005); Catherine Malabou, *The Future of Hegel: Plasticity, Temporality, and Dialectic*, trans. Lisabeth During (New York: Routledge, 2005).

31. His tour-de-force in this regard is arguably his explanation of Lacan's 'graph of desire' in *Sublime Object* (100–24), which translates one of Lacan's most complex diagrams into clear expository prose.
32. See *For They Know Not*, 94, note 28.
33. More specifically, in the case of 'empty' vs. 'full' speech, Žižek makes extremely limited use of it; the 'four discourses' are a later development in Lacan's thought that presuppose an understanding of the concepts I do explain, such that interested readers should be able to pick up on them relatively easily once they get a handle on the more fundamental concepts; and I frankly find Žižek's use of the 'Lacanian triad' to be contrived and distracting the overwhelming majority of the time. Žižek's interest is in the relationship between the Symbolic (i.e., the big Other) and the Real, and his references to the Imaginary are, in my view, a more or less perfunctory 'Lacanian' gesture.
34. See Jacques Lacan, *Seminar XX (Encore): On Feminine Sexuality, the Limits of Love and Knowledge*, ed. Jacques-Alain Miller, trans. Bruce Fink (New York: Norton, 1999), *Seminar VII: The Ethics of Psychoanalysis*, ed. Jacques-Alain Miller, trans. Dennis Porter (New York: Norton, 1997), *Seminar XI: The Four Fundamental Concepts of Psychoanalysis*, ed. Jacques-Alain Miller, trans. Russell Grigg (New York: Norton, 1998), and *Écrits: The First Complete Edition in English*, trans. Bruce Fink (New York: Norton, 2005); Bruce Fink, *The Lacanian Subject* (Princeton: Princeton University Press, 1995) and *A Clinical Introduction to Lacanian Psychoanalysis: Theory and Technique* (Cambridge, MA: Harvard University Press, 1997).
35. See *Tarrying*, 26.
36. See Karl Marx, *Capital*, vol. 1, trans. Ben Fowkes (New York: Penguin, 1992); Robert C. Tucker (ed.), *The Marx-Engels Reader*, 2nd edn (New York: Norton, 1978) – the Tucker anthology includes *The Communist Manifesto* in its entirety; David Harvey, *The Limits to Capital*, 2nd edn (New York: Verso, 2006); Althusser, 'Ideology and Ideological State Apparatuses (Notes towards an Investigation)', in *Lenin and Philosophy*, 127–86; Slavoj Žižek (ed.), *Revolution at the Gates: A Selection of Writings from February to October 1917* (New York: Verso, 2002); Henry M. Christman (ed.), *Essential Works of Lenin: 'What Is to Be Done?' and Other Writings* (New York: Dover, 1987).

Chapter 1: Ideology critique
1. *Sublime Object*, 7.
2. *For They Know Not*, 2.

3. In fact, during the high point of his visibility as a political pundit in the early 2000s, his approach seemed to be working almost *too* well – after reading a rapid succession of often predictable columns commenting on seemingly every major news event, a group of friends and I made a kind of parlour game out of trying to predict what Žižek would say about the latest headlines. We were not without success.
4. In the new preface added to the second edition of *For They Know Not*, Žižek claims that *Sublime Object* was too sanguine about democracy. As with many of his claims about *Sublime Object* in that preface, Žižek's self-critique seems to be equally applicable to all the works of the early period, even though he is implicitly claiming that all the problems had cleared up by the time he wrote *For They Know Not*.
5. Although I think it is often a mistake for theologians to read philosophers only when they are talking about religion or theology, I understand that some readers may prefer to skip to the part that is more directly relevant to Žižek's use of theology. If you are one of those readers, I strongly recommend at least reading the portions of this chapter that deal with the big Other, the Real, and enjoyment – as I say above, they come back again and again, and it is very difficult to understand what Žižek is doing without having a handle on them.
6. *Sublime Object*, 1.
7. *Sublime Object*, 2–3.
8. See Louis Althusser, 'Freud and Lacan', in *Lenin and Philosophy and Other Essays*, trans. Ben Brewster (New York: Monthly Review Press, 1971), 189–219.
9. *Tarrying*, 228–30.
10. Althusser, 'Ideology and Ideological State Apparatuses (Notes towards an Investigation)', in *Lenin and Philosophy*, 127–86.
11. Althusser, 'Ideology', 135.
12. Althusser, 'Ideology', 168, and *Sublime Object*, 36–40.
13. Althusser, 'Ideology', 132–3.
14. Althusser, 'Ideology', 162.
15. Althusser, 'Ideology', 171.
16. Althusser, 'Ideology', 178–9.
17. Althusser, 'Ideology', 175.
18. Althusser, 'Ideology', 174.
19. *Tarrying*, 229–30.
20. *Sublime Object*, 31.
21. Marx expresses this in his famous formula M-C-M' – the capitalist starts with money (M), then uses that money to produce commodities (C), which he can sell for *more* money (M'). This is in contrast with a more 'traditional' economic system that he formulates as C-M-C' – I produce a commodity (for instance, shoes), which I then sell for money, so that I can buy other needed commodities (such as bread). The shift from pre-capitalist economics to capitalism is the shift from money as a tool to money as an end in itself.
22. *Sublime Object*, 43.
23. Proceeding in this order seems to me to be important for pedagogic reasons. The idea of a social level with its own relative autonomy – meaning that it is more than simply the sum of individual actions – goes against some fairly

ingrained modes of thinking, which Margaret Thatcher famously summarized in her claim that 'Society doesn't exist'. On the literal level, as will become clear, Žižek would say that this is true, but the meaning of society's non-existence is very different from what Thatcher thought.
24. Althusser, 'Ideology', 143.
25. Both of which are mentioned in passing by Althusser, 'Ideology', 132 and 172, respectively.
26. This three-step argument is, incidentally, a prime example of Žižek's use of the Hegelian dialectic.
27. See *For They Know Not*, ch. 1, 'On the One'. I understand that this explanation may seem to move too quickly, but the next chapter will expound the concept of the subject in greater detail.
28. *Sublime Object*, 36.
29. *Sublime Object*, 28.
30. *Sublime Object*, 172.
31. See Ron Suskind, 'Faith, Certainty and the Presidency of George W. Bush', *New York Times Magazine*, 17 October 2004, for the original quotation. Shortly after the article appeared, most of the mainstream liberal blogs in the US prominently displayed the slogan, 'Proud member(s) of the reality-based community'.
32. *Sublime Object*, 49.
33. *For They Know Not*, 101.
34. See Rudolph Otto, *The Idea of the Holy*, trans. John W. Harvey (New York: Oxford University Press, 1958).
35. *Sublime Object*, 124.
36. *Sublime Object*, 165.
37. *Sublime Object*, 166.
38. *Tarrying*, 232.
39. *Sublime Object*, 148.
40. *For They Know Not*, 257.
41. *For They Know Not*, 257.
42. See *Sublime Object*, 48; *For They Know Not*, 18; *Tarrying*, 149 and 205 – among many other places.
43. *Sublime Object*, 49.
44. *Tarrying*, 202–3.
45. *Tarrying*, 208–10.
46. *Tarrying*, 226.
47. *Tarrying*, 234.
48. *Tarrying*, 227. See also the original introduction to *For They Know Not*.
49. *Tarrying*, 230.

Chapter 2: Subjectivity and ethics
1. See *Sublime Object*, 2–3.
2. *Tarrying*, 213.
3. *Indivisible Remainder*, 3 (my ellipses).
4. *Ticklish Subject*, 3.
5. For a good example of this basic objection, couched in slightly different terms than Žižek's, see Judith Butler, *Gender Trouble: Feminism and the Subversion of*

Identity, 10th Anniversary Edition (New York: Routledge, 1999).
6. *Tarrying*, 12.
7. *Tarrying*, 54. Here Žižek seems to be conflating the idea of the soul with the idea of free will in his second parenthetical.
8. See Immanuel Kant, *Critique of Pure Reason*, unified edition, trans. Werner S. Pluhar (Indianapolis: Hackett, 1996), 454–85.
9. See *Tarrying*, 56.
10. *Tarrying*, 55.
11. *Tarrying*, 39.
12. See *Tarrying*, 12–15.
13. In the standard reading, Descartes' methodological doubt 'hits bottom' at the point of the *cogito ergo sum*, that which cannot be doubted. In terms of Žižek's Lacanian reading, however, Descartes first has to hit the absolute 'bottom' of the pure void. The idea that the *cogito ergo sum* 'cannot' be doubted serves to cover over the initial moment where it in fact *was* doubted – after all, the only way to test whether it can be doubted or not is precisely by *doubting* it. (Although I am not a scholar of Descartes, I believe that this is at least a plausible reading of the *Meditations*.)
14. *Tarrying*, 17.
15. *Indivisible Remainder*, 36.
16. *Indivisible Remainder*, 16.
17. *Indivisible Remainder*, 23.
18. *Indivisible Remainder*, 29.
19. *Indivisible Remainder*, 21.
20. *Indivisible Remainder*, 31.
21. F. W. J. Schelling, *Die Weltalter. Fragmente. In den Urfassungen von 1811 and 1813*, ed. Manfred Schröter (Munich: Biederstein, 1946), 183–4; quoted in *Indivisible Remainder*, 21. Žižek's English translation is taken from Andrew Bowie, *Schelling and Modern European Philosophy* (New York: Routledge, 1993), 101.
22. *Indivisible Remainder*, 19.
23. *Indivisible Remainder*, 33.
24. *Indivisible Remainder*, 78.
25. *Indivisible Remainder*, 141.
26. *Indivisible Remainder*, 142.
27. Dietrich Bonhoeffer, *Christ the Center*, trans. Edwin H. Robertson (San Francisco: Harper, 1978), 76–82.
28. Slavoj Žižek, *Plague of Fantasies* (New York: Verso, 1997), 114.
29. *Plague of Fantasies*, 18.
30. *Plague of Fantasies*, 27.
31. See, for example, *Plague of Fantasies*, 110–11.
32. *Plague of Fantasies*, 21 (Žižek's italics removed).
33. *Indivisible Remainder*, 3.
34. *Plague of Fantasies*, 29.
35. *Tarrying*, 230.
36. *Plague of Fantasies*, 54.
37. *Plague of Fantasies*, 55.
38. *Plague of Fantasies*, 54.

39. An *Onion* article perfectly encapsulates this logic: 'Man Ashamed of Own Joy Upon Receiving New Mop Head', *The Onion*, 27 September 2000, <http://www.theonion.com/content/node/38696> (accessed 29 July 2007).
40. *Plague of Fantasies*, 188. This page contains one of Žižek's most controversial assertions, namely, that many women fantasize about being raped. He argues that 'this fact not only in no way legitimizes actual rape – it makes it even more violent', because it brutally lays bare the inmost kernel of the woman's *jouissance*, resulting in 'the worst, most humiliating kind of violence, a violence which undermines the very basis of my identity'. For me, this passage is deeply problematic on many levels, but the most fundamental issue here is whether Žižek has the right to expose this supposed 'hidden *jouissance*' of women (even if we grant for the sake of argument that such fantasies are widespread, itself a highly questionable proposition).
41. *Tarrying*, 69.
42. See *Sublime Object*, 2–3.
43. This is the subtitle of *The Puppet and the Dwarf*.
44. *Ticklish Subject*, 248.
45. *Plague of Fantasies*, 14.
46. *Ticklish Subject*, 247.
47. In fact, Žižek argues that there is no necessary relation between homosexual practice and perversion as a subjective stance – a homosexual could just as well be a hysteric. It's not a matter of content, but of form. *Ticklish Subject*, 249.
48. One of Žižek's most extended discussions of Stalinism can be found in *Did Somebody Say Totalitarianism? Five Interventions in the (Mis)use of a Notion* (New York: Verso, 2001), ch. 3: 'When the Party Commits Suicide'. Virtually all of his books have some reference to Stalinism, but other lengthy discussions can be found in *The Plague of Fantasies*, *The Puppet and the Dwarf* and *The Parallax View*.
49. *Plague of Fantasies*, 57.
50. *Tarrying*, 70.
51. *Ticklish Subject*, 297.
52. *Ticklish Subject*, 230.
53. See *Sublime Object*, 131–3.
54. *Indivisible Remainder*, 36.
55. *Indivisible Remainder*, 144.
56. In other words, the choice of the fundamental fantasy, as of the cure, reveals 'a radical split – an ontological incompatibility, even – between consciousness and freedom [. . .]'. *Indivisible Remainder*, 18 (my ellipses).
57. *Ticklish Subject*, 307, note 25.
58. See *Indivisible Remainder*, 115–17.
59. Luke 16.1–9 (NRSV).
60. Luke 16.4 (NRSV).

Chapter 3: The Christian experience
1. See, for instance, *Fragile Absolute*, 120 and 123.
2. *On Belief*, 67.
3. *Puppet and the Dwarf*, ch. 1, 'When East Meets West'.
4. Alain Badiou, *Saint Paul: The Foundation of Universalism*, trans. Ray Brassier

(Stanford: Stanford University Press, 2003).
5. *Indivisible Remainder*, 133.
6. *Puppet and the Dwarf*, 6.
7. Walter Benjamin, 'Theses on the Philosophy of History', in *Illuminations*, ed. Hannah Arendt, trans. Harry Zohn (New York: Schocken, 1968), 253–64.
8. *Sublime Object*, 131–49.
9. *Sublime Object*, 136.
10. *Sublime Object*, 138.
11. *Sublime Object*, 139.
12. *Sublime Object*, 139.
13. Benjamin, 'Theses', 253; quoted in *Sublime Object*, 136.
14. *Puppet and the Dwarf*, 3.
15. *Sublime Object*, 136.
16. *Sublime Object*, 143.
17. *Sublime Object*, 142.
18. *Sublime Object*, 137.
19. *Sublime Object*, 147.
20. *Parallax View*, 3.
21. Stuart Jeffries, 'Did Stalin's killers liquidate Walter Benjamin?', *The Observer*, 8 July 2001.
22. *Indivisible Remainder*, 36.
23. *Indivisible Remainder*, 9.
24. *Indivisible Remainder*, 7.
25. See *Tarrying*, 3–4. 'Post-postmodern' is my own term, not Žižek's.
26. Žižek deals with this issue at length in *Did Somebody Say Totalitarianism?*
27. *Ticklish Subject*, 4.
28. *Ticklish Subject*, 3.
29. Žižek's own presentation of Badiou's theory is actually one of the clearest I've read. See *Ticklish Subject*, ch. 3, 'The Politics of Truth, or, Alain Badiou as a Reader of St. Paul'.
30. *Ticklish Subject*, 142–3.
31. *Ticklish Subject*, 145.
32. See Jacques Lacan, *The Seminar of Jacques Lacan, Book VII: The Ethics of Psychoanalysis, 1959–1960*, ed. Jacques-Alain Miller, trans. Dennis Porter (New York: Norton, 1992), 83.
33. Romans 7.7–11 (NRSV).
34. For a lengthier discussion of Badiou's own reading of Paul and a presentation of Žižek's work on Christianity specifically geared toward his understanding of Paul, see Adam Kotsko, 'Politics and Perversion: Situating Žižek's Paul', *Journal of Cultural and Religious Theory* (forthcoming), <http://www.jcrt.org/>.
35. *Ticklish Subject*, 148.
36. Romans 3.8 (NRSV).
37. See Jacques Lacan, *Encore, the Seminar of Jacques Lacan, Book XX: On Feminine Sexuality, the Limits of Love and Knowledge (1972–73)*, ed. Jacques-Alain Miller, trans. Bruce Fink (New York: Norton, 1998).
38. *Ticklish Subject*, 153.
39. *Ticklish Subject*, 154.

40. *Ticklish Subject*, 162–3.
41. *Ticklish Subject*, 165.
42. *Ticklish Subject*, 211.
43. Badiou, *Saint Paul*, 10.
44. Badiou, *Saint Paul*, 11.
45. *Puppet and the Dwarf*, 53.
46. *Puppet and the Dwarf*, 68.
47. The Associated Press, 'Excerpt from Santorum Interview', *USATODAY.com*, 23 April 2003, <http://www.usatoday.com/news/washington/2003-04-23-santorum-excerpt_x.htm> (accessed 8 August 2007).
48. *Indivisible Remainder*, 118.
49. *Puppet and the Dwarf*, 54–6; *Indivisible Remainder*, 119.
50. See, for instance, *Fragile Absolute*, 120 and 123.
51. *Puppet and the Dwarf*, 27–33. This entire section strikes me as an unfairly one-sided presentation.
52. *Puppet and the Dwarf*, ch. 2, 'The Thrilling Romance of Orthodoxy'.
53. *Puppet and the Dwarf*, 37.
54. *Puppet and the Dwarf*, 53. This turn of phrase is meant to evoke 'really existing socialism'.
55. *Puppet and the Dwarf*, 57, quoting Chesterton.
56. *Puppet and the Dwarf*, 57 (my ellipses).
57. *Puppet and the Dwarf*, 97.
58. *Puppet and the Dwarf*, 15. This draws on Žižek's previous discussions of the philosopher Malebranche, who proposed that God incited Adam and Eve to sin in order to be able to redeem them. See *Plague of Fantasies*, 78–9, and *The Ticklish Subject*, 116–19.
59. See Badiou, *Saint Paul*, ch. 7, 'Paul Against the Law'.
60. Badiou, *Saint Paul*, 89.
61. Sigmund Freud, *Moses and Monotheism*, trans. Katherine Jones (New York: Vintage, 1955).
62. Freud, *Moses*, 74–5.
63. Freud, *Moses*, 113.
64. Freud, *Moses*, 115.
65. *On Belief*, 127.
66. *On Belief*, 137. See also *Fragile Absolute*, 64.
67. See the passage, discussed below, in which Žižek claims that all communities before the advent of Christianity were grounded in 'the mechanism described by Freud in *Totem and Taboo* and *Moses and Monotheism* (the shared guilt of parricide)' (*Puppet and the Dwarf*, 130). Žižek also pairs *Totem and Taboo* and *Moses and Monotheism* as equivalent in *Ticklish Subject*, 162.
68. *Puppet and the Dwarf*, 124 (my ellipses).
69. *Puppet and the Dwarf*, 125.
70. *Puppet and the Dwarf*, 125. Here Žižek is apparently ignoring the mysterious fourth figure, Elihu, who enters the scene after Eliphaz, Bildad and Zophar have concluded their speeches but before God appears.
71. *Puppet and the Dwarf*, 126–7.
72. *Puppet and the Dwarf*, 129.
73. *Puppet and the Dwarf*, 128.

74. Eric Santner, *On the Psychotheology of Everyday Life: Reflections on Freud and Rosenzweig* (Chicago: University of Chicago Press, 2001).
75. *Puppet and the Dwarf*, 119.
76. *Parallax View*, 427, note 55.
77. Krister Stendahl, *Paul among Jews and Gentiles* (Minneapolis: Fortress, 1976), 9.
78. *Puppet and the Dwarf*, 10.
79. Stendahl, *Paul among Jews and Gentiles*, 9.
80. *Puppet and the Dwarf*, 113.
81. Stendahl, *Paul among Jews and Gentiles*, 80.
82. Origen, *Commentary on the Epistle to the Romans*, 2 vols, trans. Thomas P. Scheck (Washington, DC: Catholic University of America Press, 2001 and 2002), VI.10.2. It should be pointed out that for Stendahl, the standard reading of Romans 7 stems from the well-known psychological turmoil of St Augustine, who reappropriated Paul's text for his own purposes, foreshadowing Luther's later reading of the same passage.
83. *Puppet and the Dwarf*, 113 (Žižek's italics removed).
84. Quoted in *Puppet and the Dwarf*, 14.
85. *For They Know Not*, 29 and 78.
86. 1 Corinthians 7.29–31 (NRSV).
87. *Puppet and the Dwarf*, 112.
88. *Puppet and the Dwarf*, 129.
89. *Puppet and the Dwarf*, 130.
90. *Fragile Absolute*, 120.
91. Galatians 3.28 (NRSV).
92. *Fragile Absolute*, 139.
93. *On Belief*, 91.
94. *Puppet and the Dwarf*, 102–3.
95. *Puppet and the Dwarf*, 110.
96. *Puppet and the Dwarf*, 171.
97. *Puppet and the Dwarf*, 6.

Chapter 4: Dialectical materialism, or the philosophy of freedom
1. See in particular Alfred North Whitehead, *Process and Reality: An Essay in Cosmology*, ed. David Ray Griffin and Donald W. Sherburne (New York: Free Press, 1978).
2. *Parallax View*, 168.
3. *Indivisible Remainder*, 110.
4. *Indivisible Remainder*, 74.
5. *Indivisible Remainder*, 16.
6. *Indivisible Remainder*, 226 (my ellipses).
7. *Indivisible Remainder*, 231.
8. *Indivisible Remainder*, 230. I should take this opportunity to acknowledge that I am a student of theology rather than physics and that here I am merely summarizing Žižek's argument. I have, however, discussed Žižek's work on quantum physics with a variety of people and have noticed that people who object seldom object to the specific points Žižek is making, but rather to the very idea that one could make metaphysical claims based on quantum physics

- any possibility of a link between human consciousness and quantum phenomena is dismissed out of hand.
9. *Indivisible Remainder*, 230.
10. *Parallax View*, 17.
11. Žižek draws the concept of 'parallax' from Kojin Karatani and then turns it to his own purposes, meaning that the concept around which Žižek structures his text and through which Žižek begins to assert a certain degree of independence from Lacan is, ironically, drawn from another thinker. See Kojin Karatani, *Transcritique: On Kant and Marx*, trans. Sabu Kohso (Cambridge, MA: MIT Press, 2005). Another irony: Žižek mentions many movies in *The Parallax View*, but as far as I can tell never so much as alludes to Warren Beatty's 1974 thriller *The Parallax View*.
12. *Parallax View*, 164.
13. *Parallax View*, 187.
14. Cf. Žižek's discussion of Protestantism as a 'vanishing mediator' in the transition from feudalism to capitalism: 'the break of Protestantism with the medieval church does not "reflect" new social content, but is rather *the criticism of the old feudal content in the name of the radicalized version of its own ideological form*; it is this "emancipation" of the Christian form from its own social content that opens up the space for the gradual transformation of the old into the new (capitalist) content' (*For They Know Not*, 187). Žižek draws an explicit parallel between Protestantism and the social movements in Eastern Europe that brought down Real Socialism by taking its ideology literally.
15. *Parallax View*, 172.
16. *Parallax View*, 177.
17. *Parallax View*, 179.
18. *Parallax View*, 170.
19. *Parallax View*, 177.
20. *Parallax View*, 177–8 (my ellipses). Again, as with quantum physics, my training does not qualify me to assess Žižek's use of cognitive science – I can only report it and contextualize it.
21. *Parallax View*, 177.
22. Antonio Damasio, *The Feeling of What Happens: Body, Emotion and the Making of Consciousness* (New York: Vintage, 2000) and *Descartes' Error: Emotion, Reason, and the Human Brain* (New York: Quill, 1995).
23. *Parallax View*, 223 (my ellipses).
24. *Parallax View*, 223.
25. *Parallax View*, 223.
26. *Parallax View*, 224.
27. *Parallax View*, 224.
28. *Parallax View*, 225.
29. *Parallax View*, 226.
30. *Parallax View*, 230.
31. *Parallax View*, 240.
32. *Parallax View*, 231.
33. *Parallax View*, 203.
34. *Parallax View*, 241.

35. Geoffrey Miller, *The Mating Mind: How Sexual Choice Shaped the Evolution of Human Nature* (London: Vintage, 2001).
36. *Parallax View*, 247 (Žižek's ellipses).
37. *Parallax View*, 249.
38. *Parallax View*, 249.
39. *Parallax View*, 250.
40. *Parallax View*, 249.
41. *Puppet and the Dwarf*, 53.
42. *Parallax View*, 250.
43. *Indivisible Remainder*, 74.
44. *Indivisible Remainder*, 79.
45. *Indivisible Remainder*, 220.
46. Wolfhart Pannenberg, *Anthropology in Theological Perspective*, trans. Matthew J. O'Connell (Philadelphia: Westminster, 1985).
47. Pannenberg, *Anthropology*, 15–16.
48. Pannenberg, *Anthropology*, 18.
49. Pannenberg, *Anthropology*, 21.
50. Pannenberg, *Anthropology*, 57.
51. *Parallax View*, 10.
52. A full discussion of Žižek's work on Heidegger, which in my view has been too little explored to date, is tempting, but falls outside the scope of an introductory work.
53. *Parallax View*, 23.
54. *Parallax View*, 24.
55. *Parallax View*, 168.
56. See *Sublime Object*, 2–3.
57. *Parallax View*, 49 (my ellipses).
58. *Parallax View*, 75.
59. *Parallax View*, 105.
60. *Parallax View*, 85.
61. *Parallax View*, 86.
62. *Parallax View*, 86.
63. *Parallax View*, 79.
64. *Parallax View*, 75.
65. 'While it is easy to enjoy acting in an egotistic way *against* one's duty, it is, perhaps, only as a result of psychoanalytic treatment that one can acquire the capacity to enjoy *doing* one's duty; perhaps this *is* one of the definitions of the end of psychoanalysis' (*Fragile Absolute*, 141).
66. *Indivisible Remainder*, 170.
67. *Parallax View*, 90.
68. *Parallax View*, 123.
69. *Parallax View*, 382.
70. *Parallax View*, 382.
71. *Parallax View*, 383 (Žižek's ellipses).
72. *Ticklish Subject*, 74.
73. *Parallax View*, 385.
74. John 6.60 (NRSV).
75. Žižek implicitly recognizes that this is the responsibility of a political philoso-

pher insofar as he faults Hardt and Negri for failing to provide any account of the formal structure of the revolution that would bring about the rule of 'the multitude' (*Parallax View*, 264).
76. *Parallax View*, 297.
77. *Parallax View*, 257.
78. *Parallax View*, 256.
79. *Parallax View*, 267.
80. *Parallax View*, 269.
81. *Parallax View*, 269.

Chapter 5: Theological responses
1. That is to say, even if I were not writing for a series aiming to introduce philosophers to students of theology, I would have followed the same basic outline.
2. Creston Davis, John Milbank and Slavoj Žižek (eds), *Theology and the Political: The New Debate* (Durham: Duke University Press, 2005).
3. Clayton Crockett, *Interstices of the Sublime: Theology and Psychoanalytic Theory* (New York: Fordham University Press, 2007).
4. Paul Tillich, *Systematic Theology*, vol. 1 (Chicago: University of Chicago Press, 1973).
5. It is unclear exactly when Žižek envisions the betrayal of Paul's mission taking place.
6. For a recent example, see Daniel Boyarin, *A Radical Jew: Paul and the Politics of Identity* (Berkeley: University of California Press, 1994). One notable exception is Jacob Taubes; see his *Political Theology of Paul*, ed. Aleida Assmann *et al.*, trans. Dana Hollander (Stanford: Stanford University Press, 2004).
7. As I indicate in Chapter 3, it seems to me that these two prongs could be brought together more or less smoothly with a certain degree of systematization, but Žižek has not explicitly made the connection.
8. John Milbank, Catherine Pickstock and Graham Ward (eds), *Radical Orthodoxy: A New Theology* (New York: Routledge, 1999).
9. Graham Ward, *Cities of God* (New York, Routledge, 2000). Milbank also mentions Žižek in passing in a footnote to *The Word Made Strange: Theology, Language, and Culture* (Cambridge: Blackwell, 1997), making him apparently the first theologian to refer to Žižek's work in print.
10. Karl Barth, *Church Dogmatics* I.1: *The Doctrine of the Word of God*, 2nd edn, trans. G. W. Bromily, ed. G. W. Bromily and T. F. Torrance (Edinburgh: T&T Clark, 1975), xiii.
11. For my critique of Radical Orthodoxy, focused around the edited volume *Theology and the Political*, see Adam Kotsko, '"That They Might Have Ontology": Radical Orthodoxy and the New Debate', in *Political Theology* (forthcoming), along with the contributions by Nathan Kerr, Daniel Barber and Joshua Davis in the same issue.
12. Ward, *Cities of God*, 117.
13. Ward, *Cities of God*, 148.
14. Ward, *Cities of God*, 149.
15. Ward, *Cities of God*, 168. Normally Žižek is at great pains to distance himself from Derrida, but Ward's argument in favour of a connection between the

two is convincing (albeit very compressed), especially in light of Žižek's more recent claim that Derrida's notion of *différance* bears 'unprecedented materialist potential' (*Parallax View*, 11).
16. Ward, *Cities of God*, 169.
17. Ward, *Cities of God*, 150.
18. *Theology and the Political*, 22.
19. *Theology and the Political*, 39.
20. *Theology and the Political*, 43.
21. *Theology and the Political*, 393.
22. *Theology and the Political*, 400.
23. *Theology and the Political*, 421.
24. *Theology and the Political*, 423.
25. *Theology and the Political*, 422.
26. Eugene McCarraher, 'A Merry Marxy Christmas' (review of Slavoj Žižek, *The Puppet and the Dwarf: The Perverse Core of Christianity*), *In These Times*, 23 December 2003, <http://www.inthesetimes.com/ article/123/a_merry_marxy_christmas/> (accessed 15 September 2007).
27. Paul J. Griffiths, 'Christ and Critical Theory', *First Things*, August/September 2004, <http://www.firstthings.com /article.php3?id_article=372> (accessed 15 September 2007).
28. Gerald Biesecker-Mast, 'Slavoj Žižek, the Fragile Absolute, and the Anabaptist Subject', *Brethren Faith and Life* 48.3–4 (2003): 176–91.
29. Ivan Petrella (ed.), *Latin American Liberation Theology: The Next Generation* (Maryknoll: Orbis, 2005).
30. *Latin American Liberation Theology*, 138.
31. *Latin American Liberation Theology*, 50.
32. *Latin American Liberation Theology*, 51.
33. *Latin American Liberation Theology*, 53 (emphasis in original).
34. See *Tarrying*, 78–9, and *Fragile Absolute*, 152–6.
35. John D. Caputo, *The Prayers and Tears of Jacques Derrida: Religion Without Religion* (Bloomington: Indiana University Press, 1997) and *The Weakness of God: A Theology of the Event* (Bloomington: Indiana University Press, 2006).
36. Caputo, *Weakness of God*, 12.
37. The lengthiest response to Žižek is found in a footnote, where Caputo claims that 'Žižek and Badiou . . . fail to see how undecidability and a postmodern sensibility can be packed with an existential punch' (Caputo, *Weakness of God*, 318, note 5). The overall subtext of Caputo's dissatisfaction appears to have a structure parallel to the Radical Orthodox critiques: the problem with Žižek is that he is not Derridean.
38. Crockett, *Interstices*, 131.
39. Tillich, *Systematic Theology*, vol. 1, 60.
40. Tillich, *Systematic Theology*, vol. 1, 62.
41. Tillich, *Systematic Theology*, vol. 1, 62.
42. Tillich, *Systematic Theology*, vol. 1, 63. Interestingly, Tillich omits music – even classical or 'serious' music – from his list of possible sources, whereas Žižek devotes considerable attention to classical music and especially to opera in many of his works.
43. *Plague of Fantasies*, 126, note 34.

44. *Parallax View*, 100.
45. *Parallax View*, 101.
46. *Parallax View*, 101. Though Žižek does not mention the phenomenon in this context, it is worth noting the consistent effort among many on the right (and also on the pro-war left) to identify Islamist terrorism as 'Islamofascism' and to claim strong parallels between Hitler and Saddam Hussein – or more recently, Iranian president Mahmoud Ahmadinejad.
47. *Parallax View*, 101.
48. *Parallax View*, 102.
49. *Parallax View*, 103. Throughout Žižek's works, he consistently uses 'theologist' in place of 'theologian'. It's unclear to me whether it is a mistake or carries some deeper meaning, but in any case, I have changed it above to avoid unnecessary distraction.
50. *Fragile Absolute*, 2.
51. See Žižek's introduction to Mao, available online as 'Mao Zedong: The Marxist Lord of Misrule', <http://www.lacan.com/zizmaozedong.htm> (accessed 19 September 2007).
52. Žižek, 'Mao Zedong'.
53. *Fragile Absolute*, 17.
54. *Fragile Absolute*, 17.
55. The only example of such a move in the Christian tradition that I am familiar with is found within German biblical scholarship and theology around the turn of the twentieth century. Johannes Weiss pointed out the centrality of apocalyptic to Jesus's thinking and concluded that much of his teaching was therefore unusable for the modern world. Albert Schweitzer later followed up on this insight, arguing that Jesus's claims of the coming End Times were straightforwardly wrong and concluding his study of approaches to the historical Jesus with a very poetic account of Jesus as a beautiful failure. See Johannes Weiss, *Jesus' Proclamation of the Kingdom of God*, ed. and trans. Richard Hyde Hiers and David Larrimore Holland (Philadelphia: Fortress, 1971) and Albert Schweitzer, *The Quest of the Historical Jesus*, ed. John Bowden (Minneapolis: Fortress, 2001).
56. *Fragile Absolute*, 19.
57. In an interesting parallel, the capitulation of his teachers to German nationalism in the run-up to the First World War was what led Karl Barth to make his historic break with Protestant Liberalism.
58. Slavoj Žižek (ed.), *Revolution at the Gates: A Selection of Writings from February to October 1917* (New York: Verso, 2002), 11.
59. *Revolution at the Gates*, 11.
60. The most extended version of this argument can be found in *Did Somebody Say Totalitarianism?*, though the analysis of Stalinism really is all-pervasive, particularly in his most recent works.
61. *Revolution at the Gates*, 8.
62. The attack on the Greek elements of Christianity became particularly prominent in the postwar era, when the horrific consequences of anti-Semitism had shocked Christian theologians into a reassessment of the relationship of Christianity and Judaism and produced a laudable desire to privilege the Jewish aspects of the Christian heritage. Ironically, however, in Žižek's terms, the

corresponding move of scapegoating the foreign intrusion of 'Greek' thought mimics the logic of anti-Semitism.
63. *Theology and the Political*, 422.
64. I have only found one citation of Bonhoeffer in Žižek's works: in a discussion of theological responses to the Holocaust, Žižek refers to 'Dietrich Bonhoeffer's profound insight that, after *shoah*, "only a suffering God can help us now"' (*Parallax View*, 184), but the footnote reveals that he is quoting it second-hand from a reader on the Holocaust (*Parallax View*, 408, note 59).
65. My discussion here will focus on Bonhoeffer's writings rather than his life, but one can perhaps interpret his participation in the assassination plot as a true 'act' in the Žižekian sense. A committed pacifist, he sacrificed his ethical principles in joining the plot – and not only did he violate his pacifism, but in order to keep his cover, he also began to offer external signs of loyalty to the Nazi regime such as the 'Heil Hitler', even in front of the students he had taught to resist the idolatry of Hitler. Bonhoeffer's decision has been seized upon by critics of pacifism as evidence that even a dedicated pacifist acknowledges that an extreme situation may require violence, but such an interpretation neglects the fact that Bonhoeffer himself never came up with any justification for his decision to betray his principles. It was an act not 'covered' by the big Other of his moral code – and, in light of his final works, perhaps not even by God.
66. Dietrich Bonhoeffer, *Letters and Papers from Prison*, Enlarged Edition, ed. Eberhard Bethge, trans. Reginald Fuller *et al.* (New York: Simon & Schuster, 1997).
67. Bonhoeffer, *Letters and Papers*, 280.
68. Bonhoeffer, *Letters and Papers*, 280–1.
69. Bonhoeffer, *Letters and Papers*, 326.
70. Bonhoeffer, *Letters and Papers*, 329.
71. Bonhoeffer, *Letters and Papers*, 361. As indicated in note 62, Žižek quotes the final sentence of this passage approvingly.
72. Thomas J. J. Altizer, *The Gospel of Christian Atheism* (Philadelphia: Westminster, 1966).
73. Bonhoeffer, *Letters and Papers*, 361.
74. Altizer, *Gospel*, 110.
75. *Parallax View*, 187.
76. *Parallax View*, 105.
77. *Parallax View*, 110–11.
78. *Parallax View*, 105.

Index

Abraham 90, 120–2
Althusser, Louis 17, 21–28 passim, 34, 36–7, 52, 71
Altizer, Thomas J. J. 150–4
anti–Semitism 40–1, 99, 123, 126, 131, 139, 146, 169
Aristotle 25, 85
asceticism 58
atheism 2, 63, 95, 99–100, 123, 131, 135, 137, 152
Augustine 97, 133–4, 164

Badiou, Alain 1–2, 7, 17, 46, 72–3, 77–83 passim, 88–9, 109, 127, 134, 136
Barth, Karl 125, 134, 153–4
Bartleby 123–5
Benjamin, Walter 17, 74–7, 99, 123, 133
Biesecker–Mast, Gerald 138
big Other 30–31, 45, 61, 75, 128, 148–9; and modernity, 85–86; and the Pauline community, 94–9, 152; fall of, 31, 38, 42, 64–7, 72, 82; rise of, 52, 55–6, 105–8
Bonhoeffer, Dietrich 57, 150–3, 170
Buddhism 71–2, 87, 131, 139, 153
Butler, Judith 78, 155

capitalism 16, 20, 27, 33, 40–1, 78, 82–4, 87, 128, 139, 145–8, 158, 165

Caputo, John D. 140, 168
Chesterton, G. K. 10, 87, 95, 133, 153–4
class struggle 33–4, 40, 46, 63
Claudel, Paul 76
cognitive science 102, 108–11, 123
Communism 2, 16, 20, 42, 61, 63, 68, 98, 145–8
Copernicus, Nicolaus 109
Crockett, Clayton 129, 140–1
Cupitt, Don 151
cure, psychoanalytic 44, 62, 65–9, 74, 77, 82, 122, 133, 144, 161
cynicism 20, 26–8, 34, 60, 95–6

Damasio, Antonio 112–13
Darwin, Charles 109, 113
Davis, Creston 135–7
Dean, Jodi 11, 156
death drive 53–5, 65–8, 74, 79–83 passim, 102, 112–15 passim, 122–3, 137, 145
Deleuze, Gilles 134
democracy, *see* liberalism
Dennett, Daniel 111, 113–14
Derrida, Jacques 1, 77, 135, 140, 167
Descartes, René 19, 47, 51, 54, 102, 105, 121, 160
dialectic 8–12, 14, 31–2, 50, 75, 95, 105, 109, 113, 116, 152
discourse of the analyst 82–83, 98, 103, 127, 137, 152

171

Index

Engels, Friedrich 23, 147–8
evolution 113–16

fantasy 31–9 passim, 45, 54–62 passim, 66–8, 76, 82, 92–3, 102, 133, 135–6
fascism 41–2, 148, 169
feminine logic, *see* non-all
feminism 46, 125, 139
film 2–3, 14, 13, 142–4, 156
Foucault, Michel 21–2, 77
French Revolution 39
Freud, Sigmund 13, 77, 89–96 passim, 109, 112, 118, 152

German Idealism 19, 21, 43–44, 52, 55, 112; *see also* Kant, Hegel, Schelling
God, death of 85, 87, 97, 137, 149–54
Griffiths, Paul J. 138

Habermas, Jürgen 21–2
hedonism 84, 86, 126
Hegel, G. W. F., 8–21 passim, 27, 31, 39–40, 43–4, 50–51, 71, 95, 135–6; *see also* death of God, dialectic
Heidegger, Martin 78, 87, 118–19, 166
Hitchcock, Alfred 143, 156
Holocaust 61
Holy Spirit 95–9, 103, 125–8, 131, 135, 138, 152
homosexuality 62, 86, 161
Hume, David 50
hysteria 61–6, 80, 84, 90, 128

immigrants 41, 50, 142
inherent transgression 56–7, 80, 85, 89, 94
interpellation 25, 28, 36–7, 93

Iraq 37–8
Irenaeus 97

Jerome, Saint 58
Jesus Christ 9–10, 63, 68–9, 79, 88–9, 94–9, 110, 130–2, 144, 147, 151–2, 154, 169
Job 90–7 passim, 127, 131
jokes 3, 62, 142, 153–4
jouissance 35–6, 39, 41, 46, 49, 52–67 passim, 82, 85–6, 92, 96–100, 161
Judaism 71–3, 88–96 passim, 118, 126–7, 131–2, 139, 169

Kant, Immanuel 19, 46–7, 50–1, 77, 114, 122–3
Karatani, Kojin 108, 165
Kierkegaard, Søren 101, 103, 118–23 passim, 133, 147, 153–4
King, Martin Luther, Jr 60

Lacan, Jacques 13–16, 22, 29, 68, 77–9, 81, 98; Lacanian terms listed by chapter, 13–14; *see also* separate listings for individual Lacanian terms
Lenin, V. I. 16–17, 76, 98, 137, 146–8
Lewis, C. S. 133
liberalism 38–45 passim, 78, 87, 96, 139, 145
liberation theology 125, 138–9
love 80, 82, 96–100, 110, 131, 135
Luther, Martin 53, 81, 109, 133, 146, 153–4
Lynch, David 143, 156

McCarraher, Eugene 137–8
Malcolm X 139
Maldonado-Torres, Nelson 139
Mao Zedong 146

Index

Marx, Karl 16–17, 27, 29–30, 136, 146–8
Marxism 2, 16–23 passim, 34, 74, 127, 136–7, 139, 145–8, 152
masculine logic, *see* master signifier
master signifier 29–31, 38–41, 48–9, 56, 64, 72, 81, 125
Mejido, Manuel J. 138–9
Milbank, John 133–39 passim, 150
Miller, Geoffrey 115
Miller, Jacques–Alain 3, 22
Milner, Jean–Claude 126
money 27, 30, 38–9, 41, 48, 56, 158
Morrison, Toni 139
Moses 89–90, 94

nationalism 37, 41–2, 78, 84, 127
Nazism 41, 81–2, 87, 148, 150, 170
Niebuhr, Reinhold 97
non–all 49–51, 104–5, 107, 119, 126

objet petit a 36–7, 39, 54–5, 60, 65–6, 82–3, 97–8, 126, 131
obscene superego supplement 57–58, 62, 80–1, 84, 89–95 passim
obsession 61, 63–4
Origen of Alexandria 94
Otto, Rudolph 35

paganism 30, 71, 87–8, 92–93, 98–9, 132, 144
Pannenberg, Wolfhart 117–18
parallax 108–9, 118–19, 121, 165
Parallax View (film) 173
Pascal, Blaise 11, 24, 71, 133
Paul, Saint 57, 72–3, 76–89 passim, 93–8, 126, 131–3
perversion 61–4, 75–88 passim, 93, 98–9, 126, 136, 144
postmodernism 19, 22, 42, 77–8, 81, 133, 138

predestination 54, 67, 77, 101, 111
Protestantism 109–10, 132, 165
Pseudo-Dionysius the Areopagite 33
psychosis 37, 52, 61–2

quantum physics 101–2, 106–7, 114, 116

racism 41–2, 59–60, 84
Real, the 14, 75, 77, 98, 135; and the truth-event, 81, 83; as antagonism or deadlock, 31–40 passim, 46, 76, 109; as non-all, 49–51
reality-based community 32, 159
religious right 86
resurrection 79, 81, 95, 126, 137, 151
Riches, Patrick Aaron 135–7
Roman Catholicism 110, 115–16, 138

Santa Claus 94–5
Santorum, Rick 86
Scalia, Antonin 86
Schelling, F. W. J. 45, 52–4, 67–8, 73–9 passim, 95, 106–7, 109, 132, 140
Schweitzer, Albert 169
sexual difference 46, 51, 55
sinthome 65–6
Slovenia 2–3; *see also* Yugoslavia
slums 127–8
Stalin, Stalinism 16, 63, 75–6, 98–9, 145–6, 148
Star Wars prequels 143–4
Stendahl, Krister 93–4
structuralism 2, 13, 15, 29
superego, *see* obscene superego supplement
surplus-obedience 61
symptom 65–6, 68

173

Index

Taylor, Mark C. 151
Thatcher, Margaret 159
Thomas Aquinas 133–4, 36
Tillich, Paul 140–5 passim, 168
totalitarianism 21, 26, 36–40, 78, 87
truth-event 77–83 passim, 127

unplugging 92–6 passim, 126–8

'vanishing mediator' 42–6 passim, 51–2, 55–6, 64, 67–8, 72, 76, 79, 85, 165

Wagner, Richard 88
Ward, Graham 134–5, 37
Weiss, Johannes 169
Whitehead, Alfred North 101–2
Willow Creek 24
Wittgenstein, Ludwig 5, 156

Yugoslavia 2, 22, 26–7, 60; *see also* Slovenia

www.ingramcontent.com/pod-product-compliance
Lightning Source LLC
Chambersburg PA
CBHW052047300426
44117CB00012B/2010